Making Great Gingerbread Houses

Making Great Gingerbread Houses

DELICIOUS DESIGNS FROM CABINS TO CASTLES, FROM LIGHTHOUSES TO TREE HOUSES

Aaron Morgan
Paige Gilchrist

LARK BOOKS
A Division of Sterling Publishing Co., Inc.
New York / London

CHRIS BRYANT
Book and cover design, photostyling, and production

EVAN BRACKEN
Photography

HEATHER SMITH
CATHARINE SUTHERLAND
Editorial assistance

HANNES CHAREN
Illustrations
Production assistance

ORRIN LUNDGREN
Illustrations

TRISH MCCALLISTER *supplied the photos on pages 56, 57, 92, 93, and 106*

ELIZABETH M. PRIOLI *supplied the photo on page 75*

TENLEY RAE ALAIMO *supplied the photo on page 35*

Library of Congress Cataloging-in-Publication Data

Morgan, Aaron.
Making great gingerbread houses : from cabins to castles, from lighthouses to tree houses / by Aaron Morgan and Paige Gilchrist.
p. cm.
ISBN 1-57990-268-5 (pb)
1. Gingerbread houses. I. Gilchrist, Paige. II. Title.
TX771.M786 1999
745.5—dc21 99-29333
CIP

10 9 8 7 6 5 4

Published by Lark Books, a division of
Sterling Publishing Co., Inc.
387 Park Avenue South, New York, N.Y. 10016

First Paperback Edition 2001

Distributed in Canada by Sterling Publishing,
c/o Canadian Manda Group, One Atlantic Ave., Suite 105
Toronto, Ontario, Canada M6K 3E7

Distributed in the United Kingdom by GMC Distribution Services,
Castle Place, 166 High Street, Lewes, East Sussex, England BN7 1XU

Distributed in Australia by Capricorn Link (Australia) Pty Ltd.
P.O. Box 704, Windsor, NSW 2756 Australia

If you have questions or comments about this book, please contact:
Lark Books
67 Broadway
Asheville, NC 28801
(828) 253-0467

Manufactured in China

ISBN 13: 978-1-57990-268-1
ISBN 10: 1-57990-268-5

For information about custom editions, special sales, premium and corporate purchases, please contact Sterling Special Sales Department at 800-805-5489 or specialsales@sterlingpub.com.

Acknowledgments

I would like to thank my extremely talented pastry staff, all of whom supported my efforts toward this book. Their hard work every day makes projects like this possible: Lance Ethridge, assistant pastry chef; Peter Hofmann, head baker; Heather McNally; Heather Gatesman; Carroll Dougall; Earl Winspear; Florindo Pizarro; Rose Gibson; John Roccaforte; Bobby Fisher; Julie Brown; and Eric Evans.

I would also like to thank Executive Chef Jeff Piccirillo for making me part of his team, Mike Pounders and his staff for making the photo shoots possible, and Dave Tomsky and Jessica Graves for help throughout the process of creating this book. Most importantly, I want to thank Yvonne, Daniel, and Schuyler for making my house a home.

AARON MORGAN

Season of Gingerbread

December winds swirl memories
Like snowflakes in my mind
Accumulating yesterdays
Drifting back through time.
A child waits impatiently
For the oven time to buzz
Smells of Christmas fill the air
The gingerbread is done.
Candy bright and colorful
Icing white as snow
A house, completely edible
To amaze both young and old.
In the center of the table
With family all around
The Christmas wait is over
The house comes crumbling down.
Ingredients so simple
Blended, rolled and baked
Transform to special memories
Carried as we age...

AARON MORGAN

Contents

INTRODUCTION *Making Art out of Dessert*

This is the book for every one of us who knows that it's really okay to play with our food!

In fact, after all those childhood years of having your creativity squelched, here's your official invitation to play with—not to mention to stretch, squish, color, and contort—some perfectly good food. Perfectly good for eating, and even better for rough-and-ready building. Making gingerbread houses is about rolling up your sleeves, squeezing dough through your fingers, pressing mounds of candy into globs of icing, and sprinkling on sparkly finishes to your heart's content. And it's just as much fun as you always knew it would be.

It's Play with an Artistic Purpose

But don't get the idea that this is going to be nothing but a messy free-for-all in your kitchen. Making and decorating gingerbread houses is sensory child's play, to be sure, but it also calls for careful shaping, precise fitting, intricate sculpting, and an artist's attention to color and detail. Still, it's impossible not to giggle a little—or a lot—when all this concentration is focused on marshmallows impaled on pretzel sticks, gumdrops suspended from strands of dried pasta, and Tootsie Rolls that have been softened and shaped into winter woodland creatures. Let's face it: This is happy R&R.

It's Homespun Cheer

Not only that, it's homemade holiday cheer. The process of making a gingerbread house begins with baking—filling your home with some of the most beloved scents of the season: molasses, cinnamon, ginger, cloves. Think of the warm blend wafting from your oven as aromatherapy aimed at countering the effects of shopping malls and traffic. Think of it as the opposite of pre-packaged and mass-produced.

The holiday cheer is communal fun, too. Whether there's dough to be kneaded or roof pieces to be placed at tricky angles, the more hands, the merrier. Grown-up, experienced hands. Tiny, I've-never-used-a-rolling-pin-before-but-I-want-to-help hands. Hands from next door and the hands of visiting relatives. Think of building a gingerbread house as a back-to-basics opportunity for group bonding. Think of it as the perfect excuse for downtime with family and friends at the holidays.

It's Doable

Downtime, you ask. The moments of cheer and togetherness sound good, but isn't this really an elaborate undertaking that's going to require all kinds of specialized equipment and culinary expertise? Not necessarily.

Here's what you *don't* need in order to make a great gingerbread house: expensive, house-shaped baking pans you never knew existed (they don't); a huge, commercial oven capable of baking a whole house all at once; a degree in architecture or culinary arts.

Here's what it's very nice to have: a pastry chef with an extensive gingerbread background who will take you step by photographic step through every detail of the process. And that's where this book comes in.

We give you complete, easy-to-follow instructions, all illustrated with how-to photos, for creating a basic gingerbread house pattern, cutting and baking your house pieces, and assembling the ingredients into a sturdy, standing structure. Then, with your bare gingerbread canvas before you, you can flip to our detailed section on decorating, which demystifies the secrets of gingerbread housing, from creating colored candy windows to shingling a roof.

You get contest-quality recipes for gingerbread dough and royal icing (the "glue" that holds the house together). We tell you how to make moldable candy mixtures to shape flourishes that, before this book, may have looked impossible to create in a home kitchen. And we give you a crash course in the art of viewing food as landscaping and building material, showing you how ice cream cones become evergreens, candy canes double as porch pillars, and more.

Finally, to feed your hunger for inspiring examples, the heart of the book is a bountiful smorgasbord of good ideas. Make your way down the buffet table of 40-plus houses, which have all been featured at the renowned Grove Park Inn competition, taking note of the highlighted tips and techniques for each. For more complicated features, designers have even provided detailed steps and templates you can reproduce. Mix it all together, and you've got piles of ideas supported by all the basics you need to build on them.

It's Your Chance

So, if you've lived the life of a misunderstood artist since those early days of plunging your fingers into your food, now is your chance to get some respect. Go ahead, show them all that you can create a work of art out of something those less enlightened think of only as dessert.

Gingerbread Baking and Building Basics

Mystified by the fact that gingerbread houses stand at all? Doubtful that you'd know where to begin to decorate yours, even if it was standing? Worst of all, worried that you should have started in July if you want a gingerbread house centerpiece on your table in December? This chapter is for you. Following are illustrated steps designed to take the mystery out of the gingerbread baking and building process—without entirely removing the magic.

Gingerbread house pattern pieces

THE PIECES

In this section, we take you through all the steps of creating the basic house you see pictured on the facing page. Templates you can reproduce for the entire structure, including the chimney and porch, appear on pages 112–114.

Chances are, you'll enjoy the experience of baking and building a gingerbread house most if you can spread it out over several days. Here's a rough schedule.

Allow 30 minutes for mixing your dough, plus at least three hours more to refrigerate it.
Plan two hours for rolling, cutting, and baking the dough, and another four hours for letting it cool.
Budget about an hour and a half for assembling your house, including time for it to dry and settle between stages.

Finally, some people spend several hours decorating; others garnish and adorn for weeks. Either approach is acceptable, and either way, imagination is much more valuable at this stage than expensive embellishments. Some award-winning gingerbread house builders say they come up with their best creations using little more than what they find in their kitchen cupboards. Relax: We've supplied plenty of full-color examples of what they mean by that. In fact, relax in general, and remember that ordinary people have been building with gingerbread for generations.

CREATING YOUR PATTERN PIECES

WHAT YOU WILL NEED

Pencil
Pen
Ruler or straightedge
Graph paper (optional)
Cardboard or other sturdy material (such as poster board or file folders)
Tape

If you're heading into this wondering how lumps of dough and mounds of icing will eventually transform themselves into roof peaks, window openings, and (most critical) standing walls, the answer is simple. The same way a formless piece of crepe de chine whips itself into a cocktail dress—basically. It all starts with a pattern.

We've provided one (templates begin on page 112) for a basic house, along with a porch and a chimney. Together, they create a structure that is 9 x 9 inches (22.5 x 22.5 cm) at the base and stands about 10 inches (25 cm) tall from the bottom of the porch to the tip of the chimney. The design is both manageable for beginners and full of features that allow for lots of original decorating touches. It's also easy to adapt if you've got something different in mind but want a starting point.

Simply trace the templates onto cardboard or any other stiff material, and cut them out. If you're adapting the templates or creating something different, you may want to measure your pieces on graph paper first, then create them on a stiffer paper. Then—and this step is important—construct your house out of cardboard and masking tape before you even think about dough and icing. Yes, we sound like a nagging piano teacher telling you you've got to practice your scales before breaking into your original jazz number, but trust us. When you're up to your elbows in icing trying to fit a fussy chimney piece into place, it will be comforting to draw on the memory that your pattern does fit together the way it's supposed to.

ROLLING OUT THE DOUGH

WHAT YOU WILL NEED

Flat surface

Rolling pin

Flour

Baking-grade parchment paper (you can use aluminum foil as a substitute)

Gingerbread dough

A baking board is ideal, but any clean flat surface will do for rolling out your dough. Cover your surface with parchment paper, place a portion of dough on top of it, and begin rolling out the dough with a floured rolling pin. Roll out a portion large enough for a couple of pattern pieces at a time.

Two things to keep in mind:

1 You want the dough piece you're rolling out to be as square and even as possible—and slightly larger than the pattern pieces you plan to cut from it.

2 Your rolled-out dough should be approximately ½ inch (1.3 cm) thick if your goal is stability. For accent pieces (not the main supporting walls of your house), you can roll the dough a bit thinner if you want a more delicate look.

Use plenty of flour as you roll out the dough.

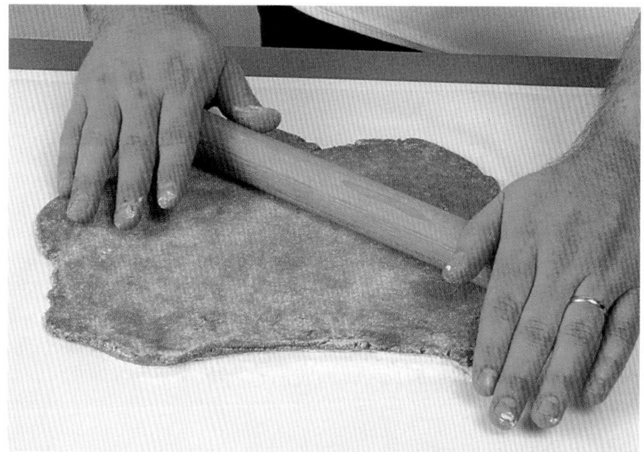

Roll gingerbread slightly larger than the pattern pieces.

Tips

BEFORE beginning your house, bake a batch of gingerbread cookies to test your dough recipe and become familiar with working with gingerbread. **—Bill Bena**

THE colder your dough, the better it will retain its shape. Leave any dough you're not working with in the refrigerator until you're ready to roll it out.

USE plenty of flour as you roll out the dough. The more you work with it, the softer—and stickier—the dough gets.

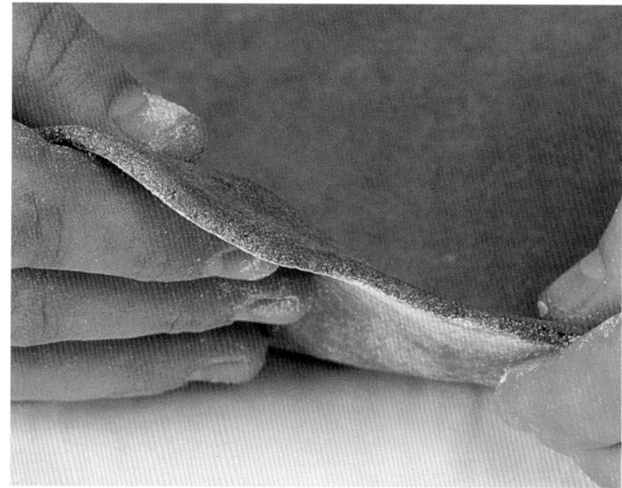

Roll dough to ½-inch (1.3 cm) thick for main supporting walls.

CUTTING OUT YOUR HOUSE

WHAT YOU WILL NEED

Flour
Gingerbread house pattern pieces
Pizza wheel
Small paring knife
Pastry brush
Airtight container for excess dough

Lightly dust the surface of your dough with flour to prevent the pattern pieces from sticking. Then, place as many pattern pieces as will fit on your rolled-out dough and, using the patterns as a guide, begin cutting your dough pieces. A floured pizza wheel works best on larger pieces, since knives can drag and misshape the dough. A small paring knife is perfect for smaller pieces and more intricate cuts, such as those on the chimney. Peel away your excess dough and save it in an airtight container. It will come in handy for creating decorations or, better yet, for a batch of cookies when you need fortitude later.

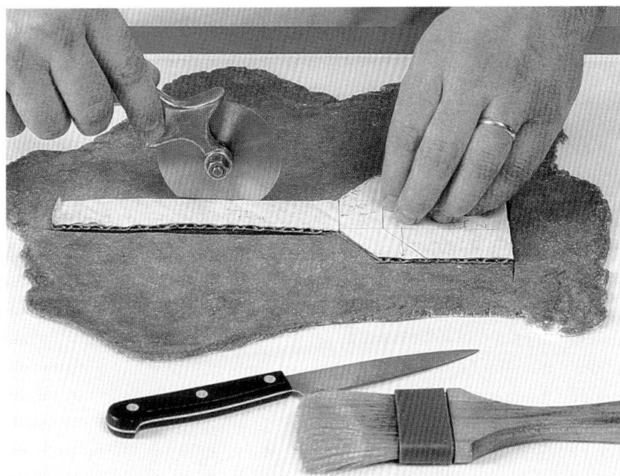

A floured pizza wheel works best on larger pieces.

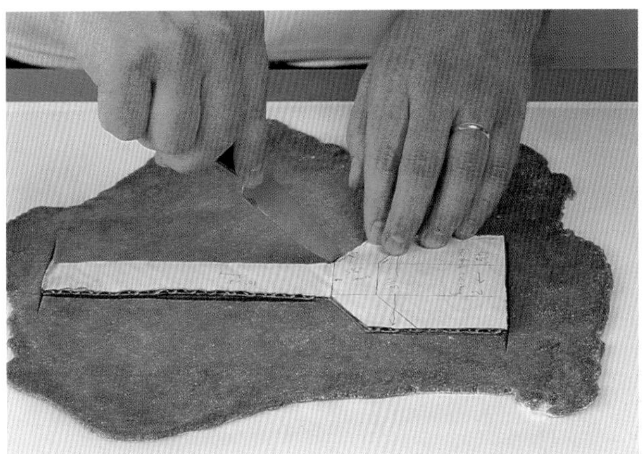

A small paring knife works well on smaller pieces and intricate cuts.

Tips

USE a pastry brush to dust any excess flour off the dough before baking it, otherwise the flour will cake on.

IF you've got time, after you've cut out your dough pieces, let them sit out, uncovered, for several days before you bake them. The settling process helps them retain their shape once you bake them. **—Judy Searcy**

Decorating Details

YOU can score or texturize pieces of unbaked dough so they resemble bricks, wooden planks, or other building materials. To make colored pieces, you can also brush liquid food coloring, watered-down gel coloring, or food coloring paste mixed with water on the dough before baking it. For example, by scoring your chimney piece and coloring it red, you can create a brick chimney effect. (For examples of this technique, see the Sweet Shop and Florist on page 76 and the Little Red Schoolhouse on page 82.)

FOR the basic house pattern we're building in this chapter, you'll need two 4-inch-tall (10 cm) supports for your porch. Peppermint sticks and other candies are options, or you may want to create gingerbread columns. If so, hand roll two ½-inch-thick (1.3 cm) pieces in the shape of bread sticks.

TRANSFERRING AND BAKING YOUR HOUSE PIECES

WHAT YOU WILL NEED

Scissors

Flat cookie sheets

Cut the parchment paper around your individual house pieces, and transfer them—paper and all—to flat cookie sheets. Space your pieces so they're about an inch (2.5 cm) apart, trying to keep larger pieces and smaller pieces on separate trays, since they may finish baking at different times.

Bake the gingerbread in an oven preheated to 350°F (177°C) until the dough is deep brown but not black (approximately 20 minutes). If you decide your pieces aren't quite done after they've cooled, stick them back in the oven for a few minutes.

Remove the cookie sheets from the oven, and allow the pieces to cool approximately 25 minutes before transferring them to a *flat* countertop or board. (If the surface is uneven, it could cause the pieces to crack or break.) Allow the pieces to cool for four hours minimum (overnight if possible) before beginning to assemble your house.

SOFT gingerbread will sabotage your house-building efforts. Bake your dough until it's completely dry and crisp.

USE completely flat cookie sheets. If they're bowed, they could cause your pieces to break.

WE recommend cutting your house pieces before you bake them (rather than baking a flat sheet of dough and cutting the pieces out of the warm, baked gingerbread). But you can do some quick nips and tucks to the just-from-the-oven gingerbread. Place your templates back on top of the warm pieces to see if the dough expanded while baking, and trim them back into shape if necessary. You could also save some of the intricate cuts, such as windows and doors, for this stage.

ALWAYS leave your gingerbread in the oven a little longer than the recipe says, even if it smells like it's burning, just to make sure it's extra hard. **—Kristen Cook**

Decorating Detail

IF you want your house to have a rougher, more textured look, use the sides of the pieces that baked against the cookie sheet as the outside of your house.

The Edibility Issue

One of the most commonly asked questions about gingerbread houses is: Can you really eat them? The answer you're likely to get from anyone who has put the time and effort into making one is: Yes, but don't you dare dig into mine.

The tradition behind gingerbread houses is that they're made entirely out of items you can eat, from the gingerbread and icing structure to the candy trim. But since so much work goes into them (and because many of the ingredients lose their freshness during the assembly process), people seldom see gingerbread houses as something to snack on. Typically, they're left intact as holiday centerpieces.

Purists (or those entering contests with food-only rules, like the one at the Grove Park Inn) are diligent about their display's edibility, down to the last candy wrapper and sucker stick (removing both). Others say it's okay to use a polystyrene base for a tree here, a piece of wood for support there, or non-food trinkets and toys for decoration all over. And those from either camp who want their house to stand for seasons to come may choose to spray the finished product with an effective but less-than-tasty coating of shellac.

THE ASSEMBLY

WHAT YOU WILL NEED

Base

Pencil

Baked house pieces, plus two 4-inch (10 cm) porch supports

Royal icing

Pastry bag and #7 plain writing tip (plus a damp cloth to keep the pastry bag covered when you're not using it)

Serrated knife

Ruler for evening up some of your pieces, if necessary

Pastry brush for dusting crumbs as you work

Several temporary braces (Spice jars, cans, or boxes of raisins will do.) (optional)

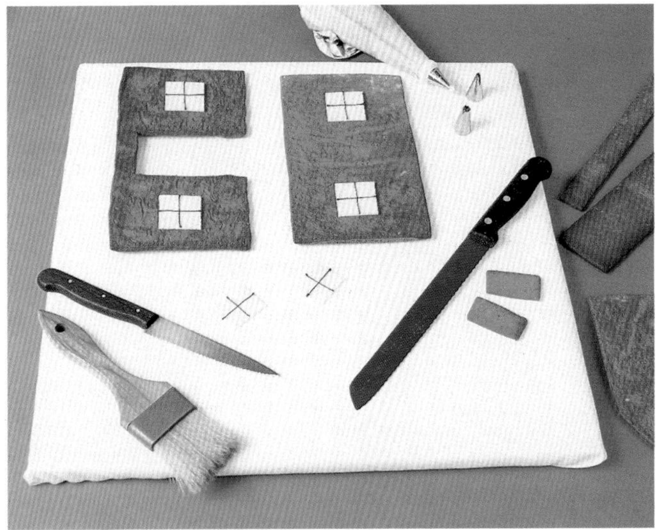

Tools for assembling your house

CHOOSING A BASE

Anything flat or sturdy will work as a base. The house we're assembling will easily fit on a large serving platter, which can be covered with frosting once your house is complete. Or, you might want to purchase a cake board (available at cake decorating shops), or cut out a wooden base and cover it with a decorative material such as gold foil. One-inch-thick (2.5 cm) polystyrene is another good choice for a base, especially if you plan to include lots of posted objects (such as candy cane trees) in your landscaping—you can stick them right in the base rather than securing them with icing. Finishing the edges of your base (by painting them to match the base surface or covering them with a decorative foil or paper, for example) lends polished appeal to your entire gingerbread display.

BEFORE YOU BEGIN

Review The Trimmings (beginning on page 20) before you start assembling your house, giving some thought to how you plan to decorate. Some of the decorating techniques, such as attaching marzipan windows or piping lattice icing on the front of the porch, are easiest if you work with flat pieces of gingerbread before they are part of the assembled house.

Piping Primer

A 12-inch (30 cm) pastry bag is a good size for both building and decorating. Fit your pastry bag with a coupler and the decorating tip you want to use, fold the sides of the bag down about one third of the way, and use a spatula to fill the bag half full with icing. Be sure to push the icing down into the tip to avoid air pockets; then twist the end of the bag to seal it. To pipe, apply pressure to the end of the bag and continue twisting it as it empties.

If you've never used a pastry bag to pipe icing before, you'll easily get the hang of brandishing it about. But don't attempt your first flourish on your house's main entrance; practice techniques and styles on a sheet of wax paper first.

BUILDING

1 Begin by lightly marking in pencil where you want the house to sit on the base. Don't forget the porch along the front. Your pattern can help you establish positions.

2 Start with the back and one side piece of your house. Pipe icing along the bottom edges, then place them over the pencil marks you made for them, forming a corner. Hold them in place several seconds until the icing begins to harden. You can also prop them in place with your temporary braces, though chances are the icing will set up so quickly this won't be necessary. See photos 1 and 2.

3 Pipe icing along the end and bottom of the other side piece and press it in place, gently holding the joints until the piece is secure. Continue until your four front and back pieces and the base of your porch are in place. Since royal icing is the glue that holds your house together, be sure to pipe a liberal amount everywhere gingerbread meets gingerbread, then go back over some of the edges, especially on the inside base of your house, for reinforcement. See photos 3–8.

4 Let your house and porch dry 30 minutes minimum—overnight if possible—before adding the roof, porch overhang, and chimney.

TO help stabilize your structure while your royal icing is drying, use straight pins or quilter's pins (which are long and have large heads) to temporarily hold your walls together. **—Sally Fredrickson**

PHOTO 1 Start with back and side piece.

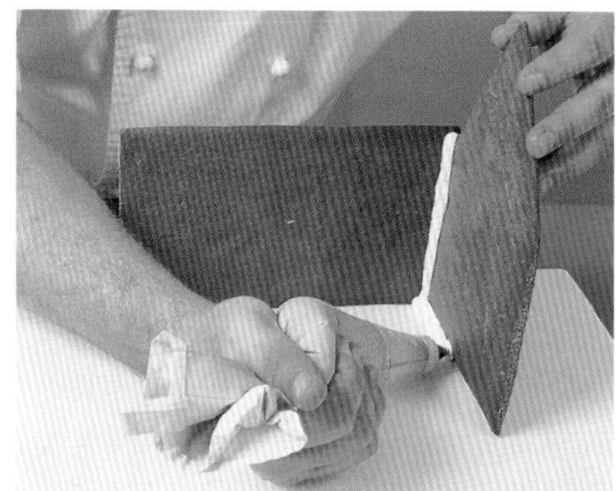

PHOTO 2 Hold and pipe pieces in place.

PHOTO 3 Add other side and front.

PHOTO 4 Attach porch sides.

PHOTO 5 Pipe additional icing.

PHOTO 6 Attach porch front.

PHOTO 7 Add porch floor.

PHOTO 8 Settle it in place.

5 Attach the porch overhang before placing the front of the roof on the house. First, position your porch supports (gingerbread columns or candy posts). If you have to shave some length off of your porch supports, use a serrated knife on the gingerbread columns or a heated knife on the candy canes. (You may want to insert the supports temporarily [to help the overhang settle into place], remove them when you decorate the front of your house, then put them back in permanently and secure them with icing.) Pipe icing along the top edge of the front house piece. Set the porch overhang in place, then attach the front of the roof, which should rest on top of the overhang. You may also need to shave your roof pieces slightly to ensure a snug fit. See photos 9–11.

6 Attach the back of the roof by piping icing along the slanted edges of the back side, then pressing the longer roof piece on the slants so that the peak is even with the front and back points. You should have a one-inch (2.5 cm) overhang in the back. See photos 12 and 13. If your roof piece needs some support to keep it from sliding as it settles, use a soda can or a box of brown sugar.

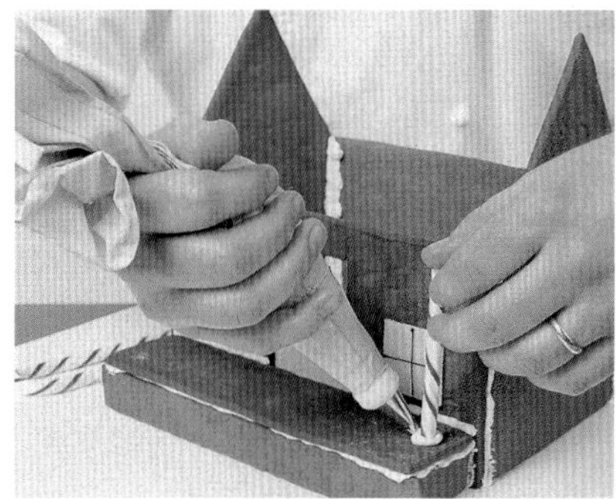

PHOTO 9 Position porch supports.

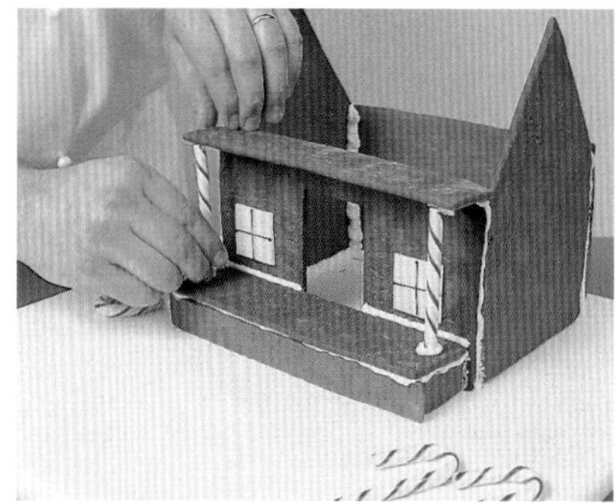

PHOTO 10 Set porch overhang in place.

PHOTO 11 Shave front roof piece, if necessary, before attaching.

PHOTO 12 Pipe icing for back roof piece.

PHOTO 13 Add back roof piece.

Tips

ALWAYS brace the insides of walls—especially tall ones—with bread sticks, thick pretzel sticks, extra pieces of gingerbread, or some other material. If your house is sturdy, you can relax and enjoy decorating. **—Elizabeth Ascik**

IF your house pieces are not fitting together evenly, use a serrated knife to straighten up your edges. Be sure to shave the pieces carefully, or more brittle pieces might break. For intricate adjustments, sandpaper or even an emery board will work well. A craft grinder is also a great tool for shaving off pieces of baked gingerbread and whittling down candy canes.

IF you're transporting your house to another location, maybe to a competition or so it can serve as a centerpiece at a party or a prize in an auction, assemble everything but the roof and fragile landscaping pieces at home; then attach the roof and finish your decorating on site, if possible.

7 To fit the chimney on the side of the house, first attach the ¾-inch-wide x 3-inch-tall (1.9 cm x 7.5 cm) side supports to the chimney face piece. Next, pipe icing along the outer edges of these lower side supports and use them to attach the chimney face to the house. Attach the ¾-inch-wide x 1½-inch-tall (1.9 cm x 3.8 cm) side supports and the 6¼-inch (15.7 cm) side supports. The notches in the longer pieces, which fit over the lip of the roof, will likely have to be shaved slightly so that they fit snugly in place. Finally, fit the tiny piece with an inverted "V" notch over the peak of the roof to form the fourth side of the chimney. See photos 14–18.

8 For each window dormer, attach two triangle pieces to the roof 1½ inches (3.8 cm) apart (the longest side attaches to the roof), and place a square piece on top of them. You can also cover the entire roof in a blanket of royal icing snow, as we did, and simply position the pieces of the window dormers in the icing. See photos 19 and 20.

JUNE SMITH and **SHANON SMITH**, who built the house on page 42 in Dallas, Texas, during two weeks of nonstop rain and 85–95 percent humidity, are experts on working with gingerbread in an especially humid climate. Their advice is to make each exterior wall of your house a double wall by icing two identical pieces of gingerbread together. The royal icing in between helps draw moisture out of both pieces of gingerbread. In addition, the double walls provide extra support for the roof.

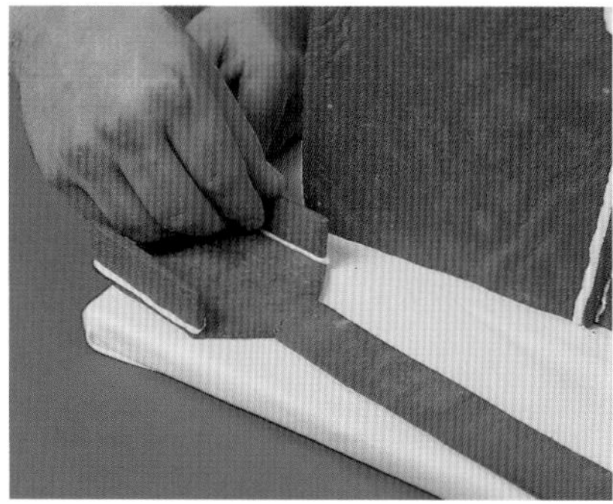

PHOTO 14 Attach lower chimney side supports.

PHOTO 15 Attach chimney to face of house.

PHOTO 16 Add middle side supports.

PHOTO 17 Attach notched side supports.

PHOTO 18 Fit tiny notched piece over roof lip.

PHOTO 19 Cover the roof with icing.

PHOTO 20 Add window dormers.

Making a Paper Piping Cone

For delicate details that require fine piping, you can either use a pastry bag and the tiniest tip you can find, or you can practice some easy kitchen origami and create your own cone. Start with parchment paper, then follow the steps shown here.

STEP 1 Fold parchment paper to create a triangle.

STEP 2 Flatten the edge with a knife.

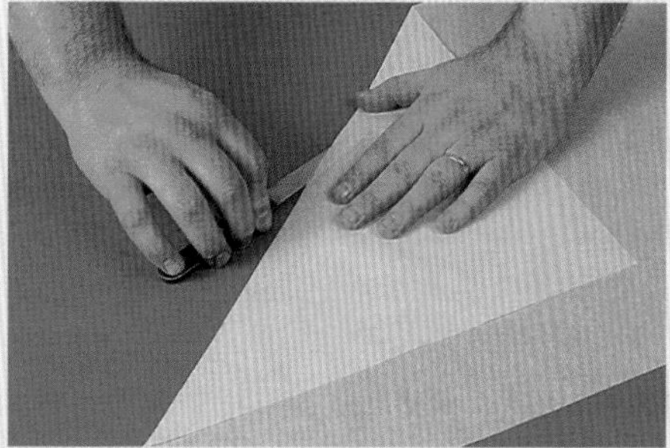

STEP 3 Cut the triangle out of the larger piece of paper.

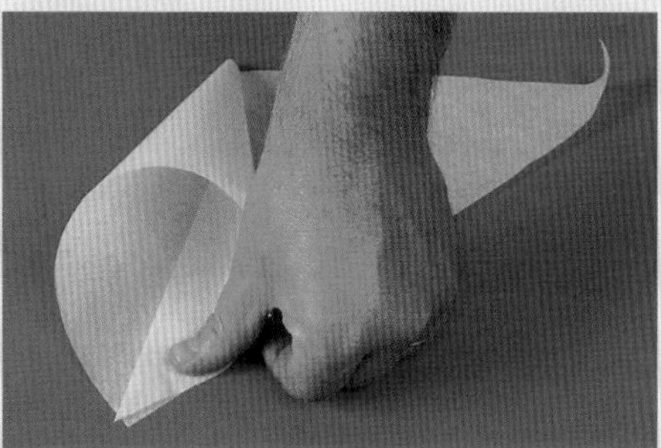

STEP 4 Bring one point from the base of the triangle up to the top point.

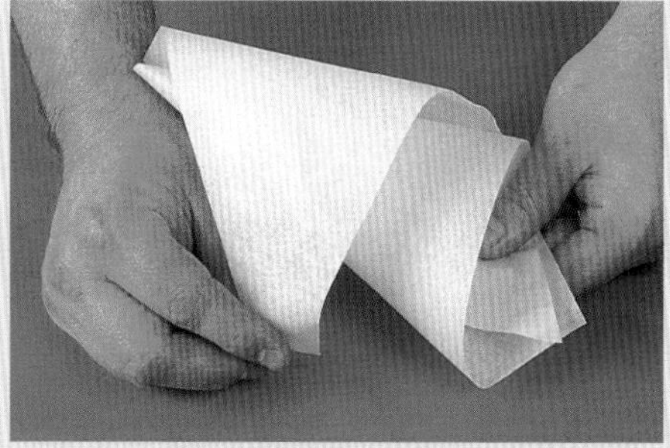

STEP 5 Wrap the other base point around and up to the back of the top point.

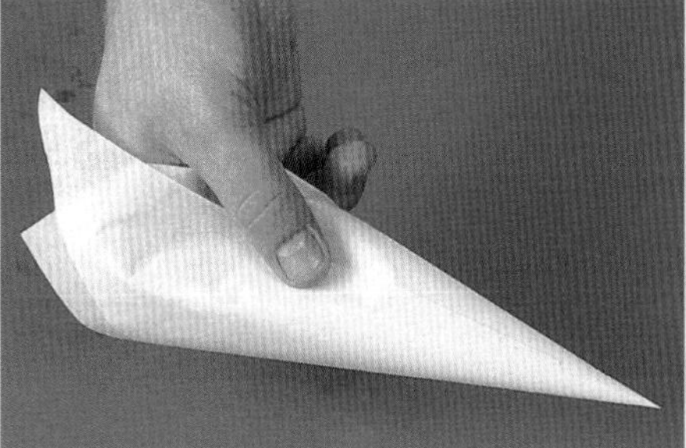

STEP 6 Shuffle the paper so that the inside piece is tightening while the outer piece continues to wrap. The action forms a tight tip.

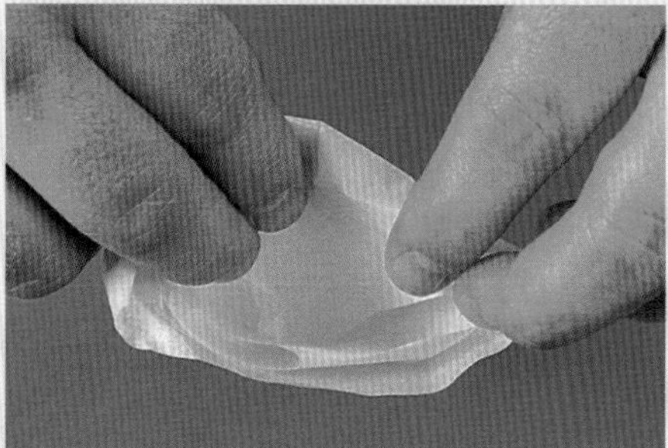

STEP 7 Fold in the pieces at the top of the cone to hold the shape in place.

THE TRIMMINGS

WHAT YOU WILL NEED

Royal icing (recipe on page 34)

Pastry bag and decorating tips (We recommend a #21 star tip, a #16 star tip, a #7 plain tip, a #2 plain tip, and a #352 leaf tip to get started.)

Damp cloth to keep pastry bag covered when you're not using it

Small, angled spatula for spreading icing

Food coloring (Food coloring comes in multiple colors and various forms, including liquid, paste, powder, and gel. Powder is best for coloring chocolates, while paste or gel is ideal for icings.)

Assortment of all things edible (Candy, crackers, cookies, cereal… you get the idea. The more unusual the better, and the more in general the merrier.)

Wax paper (optional)

Decorating supplies

Assortment of food coloring

Let's be honest. Cutting out templates and watching the walls and roofline of your gingerbread house come together may bring out the inner architect in you, but this is the part you've been waiting for. Hold back briefly. Let your newly assembled house settle for at least an hour, overnight if you can stand it. Once it's dry and stable, you're ready to start decking the halls—not to mention the walls, windows, doorways, and yard—anywhere icing will stick and some piece of food you're transforming into a shingle or stone will hold.

Schools of thought compete. Some gingerbread artisans say they scan storybooks, vintage cards, catalogues, and modern magazines before settling on a specific theme, then follow it faithfully down to the last piece of candy trim. Humbug, say others. The fun is in following a muse that makes it up as it goes along. If we've got to deal in controversy, what a happy one to have. The ideas and techniques in this section provide the basics for implementing your decorating approach, whatever it may be. Variations on these basics—from the simple to the elaborate—abound in the houses and other structures on the pages that follow.

VISIT candy stores for inspiration. Browse the aisles of the places that sell in bulk, and you're bound to leave with a new idea or two for shingling your roof (try sticks of red gum curled up at the ends), shuttering your windows (how about chocolate bars?), or even paving the path to your door (the darker colors of gourmet jelly beans make great gravel; so does sundae topping).

Attaching Necco wafers with royal icing

Roof Decor

The big open space of your roof calls out for imaginative adornment. If you want your roof to look realistic, consider crackers or shredded wheat squares for a thatched motif. Layered Necco wafers or wafer cookies are popular for creating a more colorful, shingled style. You may simply want to frost your entire roof in white royal icing and pipe a scalloped design with chocolate. Or, drip icicles from your window dormers and "let it snow."

Wafer cookies used as roofing

A thatched roof of shredded wheat squares. DESIGNER: **Elizabeth Prioli**

Icicles of royal icing dripping from the roof and dormers

Placing a marzipan window into a dormer

Attaching shutters

Adding a door made of licorice iced on a gingerbread base

Windows and Doors

You can attach window shapes to the flat house pieces before your structure is assembled, or add them once it's standing. Roll a thin layer of marzipan, and cut out shapes to fill your windows. Secure them in place with royal icing, and pipe in chocolate frames or even colored curtains or candles that look like they're positioned on the inside sill.

Most any sort of wafer cookie or thin candy bar can be used as a propped-open front door or for window shutters. You can also bake your own doors and shutters out of gingerbread, and decorate them with icing and candy.

IF high humidity moistens your gingerbread and makes it droop or causes your poured sugar windows to turn to syrup, try keeping a night-light burning inside your house 24 hours a day while you're building it to help dry it out. **—Sally Fredrickson**

Window Repairs

Candy windows can crack and break, and they're especially prone to melting in humidity. If you have to whip up a quick replacement, measure the size of your frame, then use sticks of gum, licorice, or any sticky, pliable substance to create a shape identical to your window frame. Make a small batch of poured sugar or melt crushed hard candy in the microwave, then pour the melted mixture into the temporary gum or licorice frame. Once your replacement window is hard and cool, you can peel it off the makeshift frame and ice it into its permanent position on your house.

Melted Candy Windows

To make candy windows that look like stained glass, follow the procedure shown here. First, cut out your window shapes and begin baking your gingerbread. While it's baking, use a hammer to crush colored candies in their wrappers. Remove the gingerbread piece with window openings from the oven when approximately 10 minutes of baking time remain. Fill the openings with crushed candy, bringing the candy level with the surface of the gingerbread. Stick everything back in the oven for the last 10 minutes of baking, and the candy will melt into colored glass window panes. Keep a careful watch during the final stage of baking. If left in the oven too long, the melting candy may flow out of the window openings.

Poured sugar windows are a more advanced variation on the melted candy theme. Combine 1¼ cups (250 g) of granulated sugar, ½ cup (170 g) of corn syrup and ⅓ cup (80 ml) of water in a saucepan and heat the ingredients gently, stirring constantly, until the sugar dissolves. Bring the mixture to a boil, and cook it without stirring until the temperature reaches 310°F (154°C) (using a candy thermometer to measure the temperature). With great care (and oven mitts!), pour the boiling sugar into your window forms. Kids need adult help if they're going to try this technique.

Crush colored hard candy.

Fill the window openings.

Remove stray bits of candy from gingerbread before baking.

Bake approximately 10 minutes, then cool to harden before handling.

Color Flow

For decorative surfaces with a smooth sheen (like the bright yellow windows shown here), use the color flow technique we've illustrated. Create a thin royal icing by combining a one-pound box (454 g) of confectioners' sugar, two tablespoons of meringue powder, and approximately three teaspoons of water. Beat the mixture on a low speed for about 20 minutes, adding more water as you mix if the color flow seems to be too thick. (Beating it on a low speed for a good length of time will help prevent the piped-on color flow from developing air bubbles.) When you've finished mixing, add food coloring, if you like.

With a pencil, draw the pattern you want to create on a piece of wax paper. Pipe your thin icing onto the border of your pattern first, using a #3 or #4 decorating tip or a handmade paper cone (the goal here is a thin, fine line), then fill in the interior. Let your first color dry thoroughly before adding accents in a new color. Be sure to let your entire creation dry completely (at least 48 hours), or it will crack immediately when you try to remove it from the wax paper. Even when they're dry, color flow pieces will be brittle, so handle them with care when you pick them up and ice them into place.

Pipe a thin border around your design.

Fill the interior.

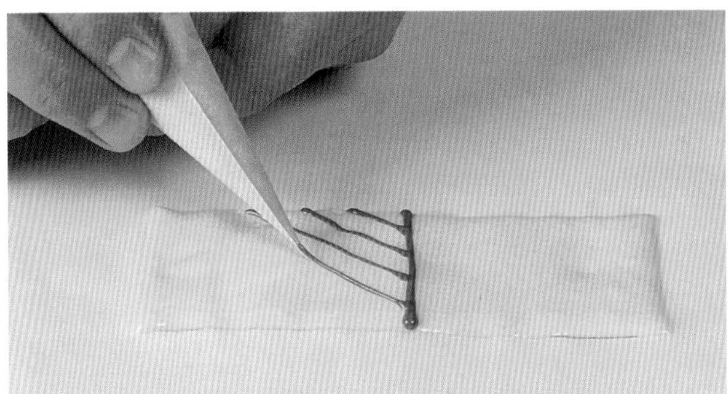

Let the first color dry thoroughly before adding another.

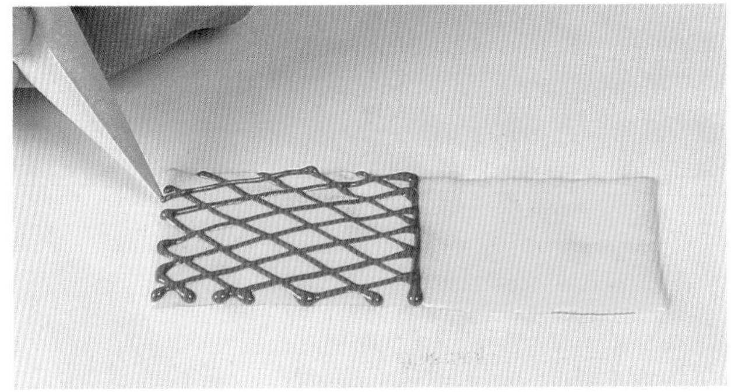

Let the entire piece dry at least 48 hours before handling.

Windows made with color flow. DESIGNER: **Kathy Moshman**

Wreaths and Garlands

With a #352 leaf tip, you can pipe colored royal icing garlands directly onto your porch—or on a fence or gate in the yard. You can also create wreaths by piping circles onto wax or parchment paper. Apply candy decorations before the icing hardens, then let the wreaths dry completely (overnight if you've got the time) before moving them from the paper to their hanging positions on the house.

Making a wreath

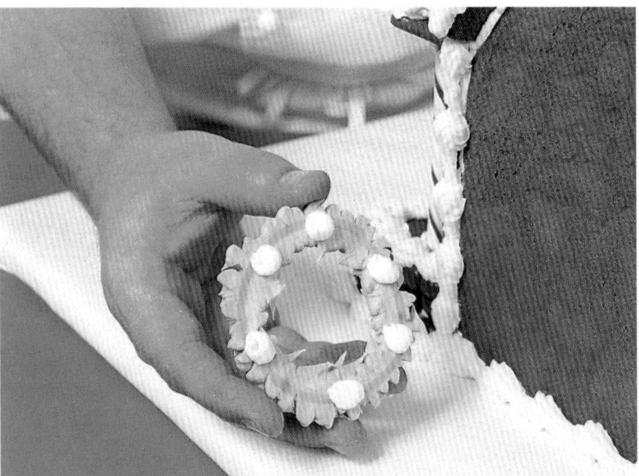

Let the wreath dry completely before handling it.

A COUPLER on your pastry bag will let you easily change icing tips to create different effects.

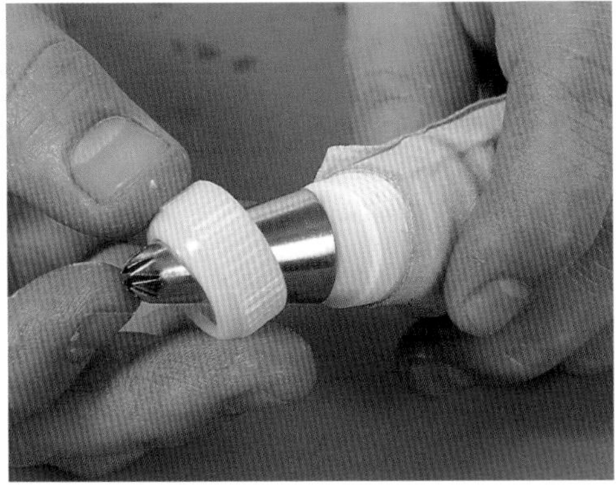

Attach the wreath with royal icing.

Icing Trim

Regardless of how you choose to decorate, piping swirls of icing along all the edges, seams, and borders of your house (from doors and windows to the edges of the roof) both provides a finished look and helps reinforce the structure. The icing tips we recommend—attached to a pastry bag—will get you started on a basic variety of decorative borders.

Icing can also be used to pipe everything from a lattice pattern on the base of your front porch or on your window shutters (it's best to do this before attaching those pieces) to icicles hanging from the roof. For the icicles, pipe a base dot, then drip the icing down from there. A #2 plain tip is good for making smaller icicles.

LEFT: Different tips create different piping designs for borders and trim.

BELOW: Icicles drip from every overhang on this turn-of-the-century inn. DESIGNER: **Kristen Cook**

Piping trim

Piping lattice

Piping icicles

Building Materials

Give yourself a little time, and you'll start to view the grocery store as a fully stocked home and building supply center. Pretzels, for example, are ideal fence-building material. Post them in mini-marshmallows, then fuse rails together with royal icing for a split-rail look. Tootsie Rolls can be softened in the microwave for a few seconds, then shaped into everything from stumps to wood piles.

You can also craft custom-designed bricks, stones, logs, and texturized surfaces out of gingerbread dough, then ice them on where you want them. Brush the building-materials-to-be with food coloring, if you like, before baking them. (The Sweet Shop and Florist design on page 76 is a marvelous example of how baked-in color can be used to create aged wood.) For a sturdy log cabin, attach rolled-dough logs to your house pieces, then bake them into place. Create a brick surface without the time-consuming task of mortaring individual pieces by scoring the dough with a knife (or using a purchased mold to make brick-like impressions) before it goes in the oven.

To create stones that will pass for real rocks, knead natural-colored marzipan with marzipan you've colored in darker shades, marbling the two together. Chocolate-covered raisins and walnut pieces work well, too.

Marzipan "stones" cover the chimney.

Chocolate-covered raisins provide facing for the foundation.

Pretzles set into mini-marshmallows make a good fence.

Creating Rounded Structures

For turrets like the ones on the Scottish Castle (page 74), rounded front windows like those on the Sweet Shop and Florist (page 76), and other rounded gingerbread structures, simply drape pieces of dough over cans (soda and coffee cans are perfect) and around pipes, then bake them into shape. Cover the base first with aluminum foil or parchment paper. (Masking tape is fine to hold the foil or paper in place. And yes, it will survive the baking process.) Then, grease the foil or paper lightly before adding the dough. You can rest the entire contraption on chopsticks so one side of your rounded structure won't flatten as it bakes.

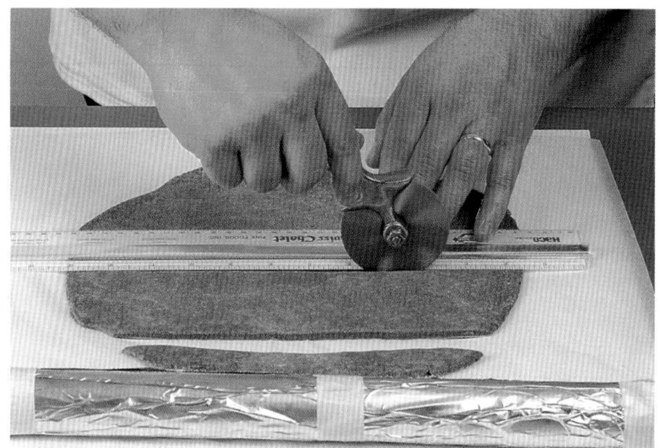

Cutting strips

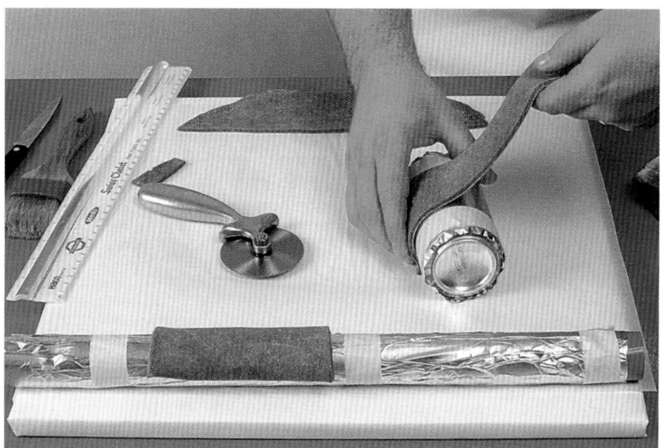

Draping strips over a foil-covered can and pipe

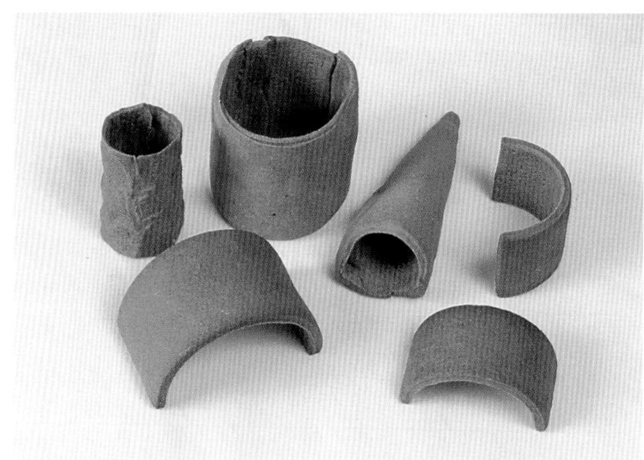

A variety of cylindrical and cone-shaped gingerbread pieces

SPRINKLE everything with confectioners' sugar when you're finished, and your entire gingerbread scene will look like it's just been dusted with snow.

Landscaping

You can take care of an afternoon's worth (or, with a little ingenuity, an entire weekend's worth) of digging, planting, mowing, and sprucing—all in the cozy comfort of your kitchen. Landscaping features have almost no limits, and they add loads of character to your gingerbread display.

Upside-down sugar cones are the perfect shape for evergreen trees. Cover them with points of green-colored royal icing (using a #352 leaf tip), and decorate them with candy ornaments such as Red Hots. If you're willing to add inedible pieces to your display, craft stores sell different sizes of polystyrene cones—good to use if you decide to create an entire forest. Or, simplify the process considerably (especially if you're going for a Hansel and Gretel candy cottage look) and stand suckers and lollipops up as instant trees. Marshmallows coated with royal icing and covered with green-colored coconut give you shrubs with plenty of texture to line a path or border a fence.

Create a skating pond by spreading waves of blue-colored royal icing on your base or by coloring corn syrup and pouring it into a bordered area. Consider lining your pond with gumdrop rocks or crumbled gingerbread gravel, and toss some sugar crystals on top for chunks of frosty ice.

For a lamppost, stick a chocolate-covered confectioners' stick in a base of royal icing, then use another drop of icing to mount a candy ball (small jawbreakers work well) on top of the stick.

And this is only the beginning. Peruse the projects on the pages that follow for ideas for making mountains, moats, and more.

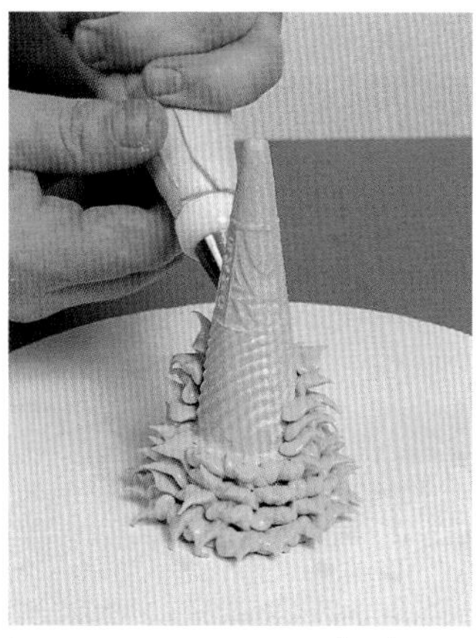

A sugar cone as an evergreen-tree base

A skating pond made of blue royal icing

This skating pond was created by crushing, then melting, blue hard candy.
DESIGNER: **Elizabeth Prioli**

These snow-covered bushes were made of royal icing, coconut, green food coloring, and oregano flakes. DESIGNER: **Elizabeth Prioli**

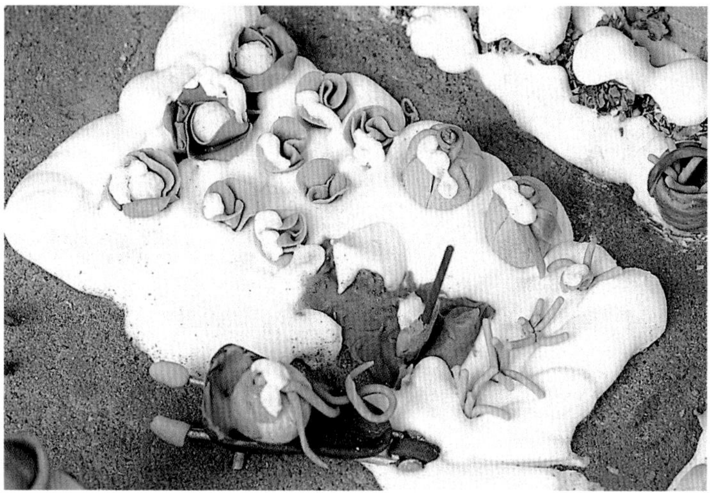

The soil in this winter garden is a mixture of nutmeg, hamburger seasoning, and royal icing.
DESIGNER: **Elizabeth Prioli**

Marzipan Figures

A bit like edible play dough, marzipan is a pliable candy that can be rolled, pressed, and molded into people, packages, and creatures great and small. It's easiest if you have several colored batches (such as brown and red in addition to natural) within reach when you're working on your figures. A recipe appears on page 34. Photos here show the steps to making a marzipan dog.

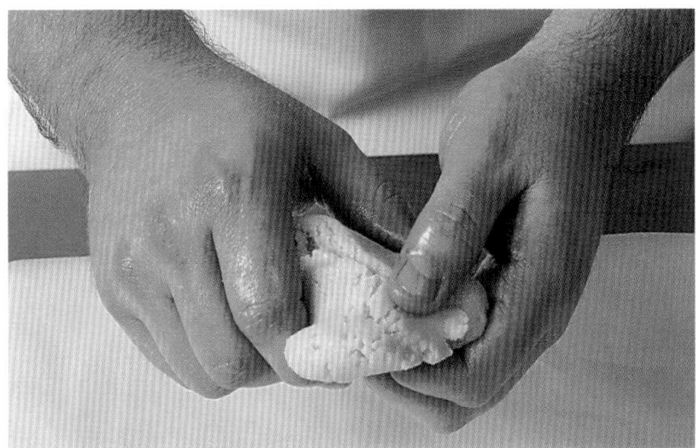

First, knead the marzipan to soften it.

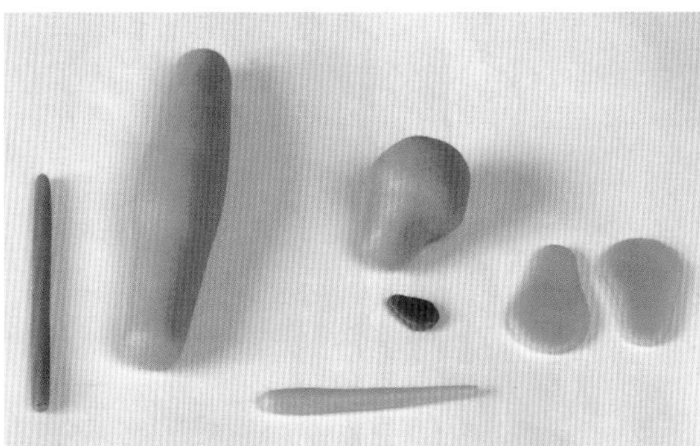

Roll out marzipan pieces for the dog's body, head, ears, tongue, tail, and collar.

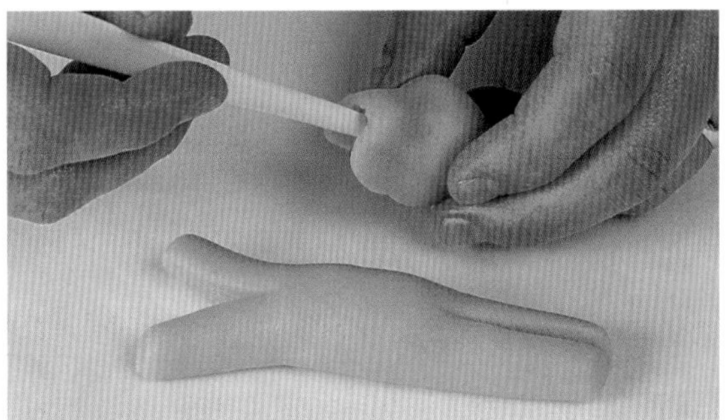

Slit both ends of the body to create front and back legs, and create a mouth on the head.

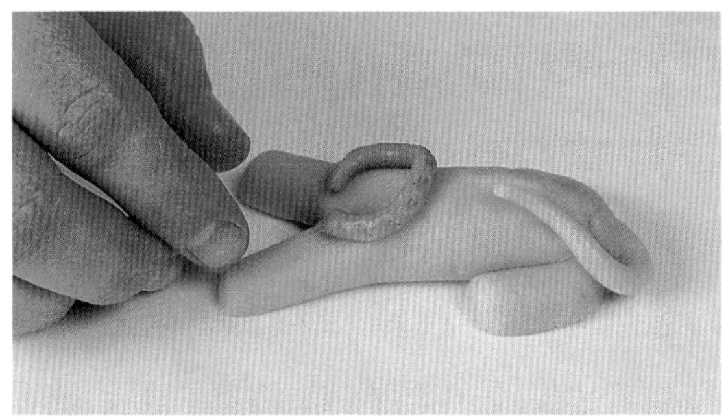

Add the tail and collar.

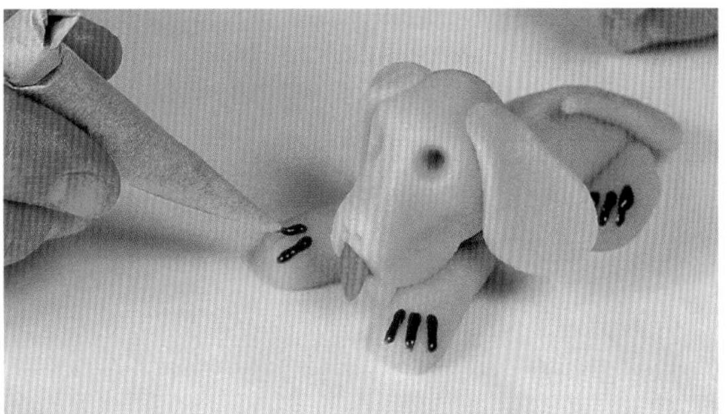

Add the tongue and ears to the head, create eyeholes, and pipe chocolate to accent the eyes, nose, and paws.

IF your display requires a lot of sculpting and molding, you might want to try rendering some of the features out of clay before struggling with marzipan or whatever material you're using.
—Hobey Ford

Pastillage Figures

Pastillage, similar to stiff putty, is sometimes referred to as gum paste. You can shape it into curving architectural structures, drape it in the form of blankets, or swirl it around a snowman's neck as a scarf. Whatever you make will harden in minutes into a durable, snow-white decoration, which you can frost, paint with food coloring, or leave as is. Best of all, pastillage is a cinch to make; follow the recipe on page 35.

These lunching ladies clothed in pastillage dine at a pastillage table.
DESIGNER: **Elizabeth Prioli**

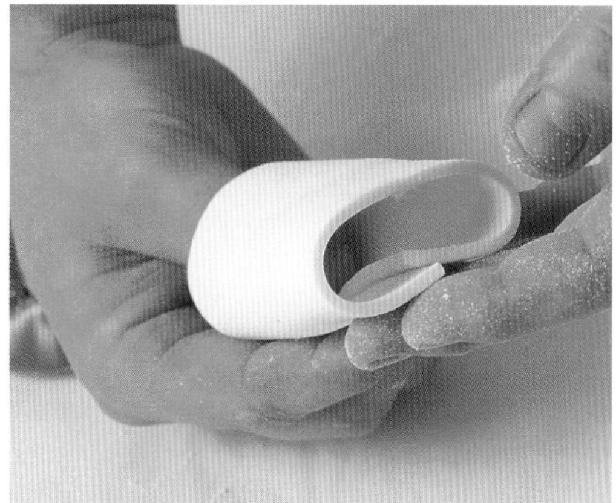

Pastillage is perfect for making curved forms and simulating draped fabric.

A napping pastillage cat on a bed of shredded wheat hay.
DESIGNER: **Elizabeth Prioli**

Pastillage drying as it is molded over a cylinder. It will harden in minutes.

A church choir decked out in pastillage. DESIGNER: **Elizabeth Prioli**

Fondant Figures

A close cousin of pastillage, fondant is also in demand for its bright white color and malleability. Unlike pastillage, however, it contains fat. While it will hold its shape (somewhat like soft clay), it will never harden into as rigid a form as pastillage will. Pre-made fondant is available at cake decorating shops (in white and various colors, flavored and unflavored). You can also make your own, using the recipe on page 35.

Fondant is malleable like pastillage, but does not harden into a rigid form.

Melted Chocolate Features

There's not much in life that can't be made better with a dose of chocolate. So it goes with gingerbread decor. Melted chocolate, which you can pour, pipe, or dip into, provides just the touch of silky luxury you may be looking for. You can get standard cooking chocolate in wafers and chunks, and in white (which can be colored to match almost any shade) and dark. It's just the thing for dipping and simple piping.

Kristen Cook used melted baking chocolate on her Avonlea Inn (page 44) to coat the porch pillars. She simply dipped bread sticks down in it. ("It provided a much smoother finish than icing.") She also put it in a pastry bag and, with a tiny tip, piped the inn's widow's walk and porch railing. To do something similar, draw the pattern you want to follow, whether it's crisscrosses or elaborate curlicues, on a sheet of white paper. Cover it with see-through wax paper, then pipe according to your design. Freeze the piped chocolate for about an hour, then carefully peel your delicate pieces off the wax paper and put them in place.

If you want to create super-sturdy, stand-alone structures (such as the gas lamp featured in the Holiday Village on page 106), you'll have the best results if you use the highest-grade chocolate ("couverture," it's called), and "temper" it properly. (Tempering is a heating and cooling process that requires a candy thermometer as a gauge and the simple instructions in a candymaking book as a guide.)

Because it contains fat, fondant is glossy.

A snowman made of fondant (left), and figures shaped of pastillage

Lighting a House

Just like real-life houses that look warm and welcoming when lights are burning inside, a gingerbread house with see-through windows and an inside light has added charm. Here's how to outfit your house with a burning bulb.

1 Think ahead. The time to decide you want to light your house from within is before you've put it together. You'll want to choose a base in which you can cut a hole and prepare it for a light set before you put up your walls.

2 Purchase an inexpensive light set at a craft shop; it will include a bulb, its base, and a cord.

3 Cut a hole in your house base to accommodate the light set. So the light cord won't prevent your base from sitting flat, you'll also want to either carve a groove along the underside of the base (easy to do if your base is polystyrene), or equip your base with feet so the cord can wind under it.

4 Once your house is assembled, insert the bulb and its base through the hole you've prepared, and plug it in.

A base equipped with a light set

The most important thing is not to rush when you're assembling and decorating your house. I always leave a few days at the end for last-minute touch-ups. Thinking up new and creative decorations is what keeps it fun. **—David Handermann**

Golden light glowing through hard-candy windows adds an inviting charm to this gingerbread church. DESIGNERS: **Thomas Marshall** AND **Jamie Merritt**

THE RECIPES

GINGERBREAD DOUGH

This recipe makes enough dough for the basic house, porch, and chimney shown on page 10. A heavy-duty mixer will ease the dough-making process. If you don't have one, put on some holiday music and prepare to enjoy the time-honored rhythms of kneading.

CREAM UNTIL LIGHT AND FLUFFY:

2 sticks (1 cup or 230 g) butter

¾ cup (100 g) firmly packed brown sugar

ADD AND BLEND ON LOW SPEED:

¾ cup (250 g) molasses

SIFT, ADD, AND BLEND UNTIL ALL THE FLOUR IS ABSORBED:

5¼ cups (630 g) all-purpose flour

2 teaspoons baking soda

2 teaspoons cinnamon

2 teaspoons ground ginger

½ teaspoon ground cloves

1 teaspoon salt

Add and blend:

¾ cup (177 ml) cold water

Spread the dough out on a sheet pan, cover it tightly with plastic wrap, and refrigerate it until you're ready to roll it out (ideally overnight; three hours minimum). It should keep well in the refrigerator for approximately three days.

Softening your butter by getting it to room temperature before beginning the creaming process will give you a helpful head start—especially if you're kneading by hand.

ROYAL ICING

You should have enough icing to construct and decorate your basic house, porch, and chimney with this recipe. However, because the icing will eventually dry out, you might make just half the recipe for constructing your house, then whip up the second half when you're ready to decorate.

5¼ cups (630 g) confectioners' sugar

1 tablespoon and 1½ teaspoons cream of tartar

½ cup egg whites (120 ml)

Sift the sugar after measuring it. Add the egg whites and cream of tartar to the sugar mixture. Combine the ingredients with a hand mixer on low speed, then beat them on high for two to five minutes, until they're snow-white and fluffy.

Keep your icing bowl covered with a damp towel to retain moisture; the mixture crusts quickly when it's exposed to air.

Royal icing is hands down the best choice for assembling and decorating gingerbread houses. Most other icings contain shortening or butter that will eventually soak into the gingerbread and could cause your house to soften and collapse.

MARZIPAN

8 ounces (237 g) almond paste (You can purchase pre-made paste in most gourmet groceries or cake decorating shops.)

2 tablespoons corn syrup

1½ cups (180 g) confectioners' sugar (sifted)

Mix the almond paste and corn syrup on low speed until they form a smooth and very tight mixture. You may have to knead the ingredients by hand to blend the mixture completely. Add sugar, a bit at a time, as fast as it's absorbed. Stop when the mixture is stiff but still workable and not too dry. If it crusts over before you use it, microwave it for a couple of seconds before you begin working with it.

Tip

Marzipan crusts over quickly, so keep it wrapped in plastic when you're not using it.

PASTILLAGE

- 1 *tablespoon gelatin*
- ¼ *cup plus 2 tablespoons (59 ml plus 2 tablespoons) water*
- 4½ *cups (540 g) confectioners' sugar*

Dissolve the gelatin in the water, then add the confectioners' sugar. Keep the mixture covered with a wet towel to prevent it from drying out. The surface may still crust a bit, so sprinkle some more confectioners' sugar in, and knead the pastillage just before using it.

FONDANT

- 8 *tablespoons (1 stick) unsalted butter*
- ¾ *teaspoon vanilla*
- ¼ *teaspoon salt*
- ⅔ *cup (225 g) sweetened condensed milk*
- 5 *cups (600 g) sifted confectioners' sugar*

Beat the first three ingredients until they're soft, then add the sweetened condensed milk slowly and beat the mixture until it's very light. Add the confectioners' sugar, cup by cup. Dust your work surface with another cup (120 g) of confectioners' sugar, turn your fondant out onto the surface, and work the sugar into it with your hands. As with pastillage, the surface of your fondant may crust as it sits. If so, sprinkle it with additional confectioners' sugar and knead it just before using it.

To Munch or Not To Munch

Gingerbread houses made for display often aren't meant to be eaten, yet they're so tempting to passersby. Tenley Rae Alaimo came up with an ingenious solution when she created this gingerbread replica of an historic house in Georgetown, New York. She turned the flat roof into a serving dish for Christmas cookies.

Houses, Cabins & Inns

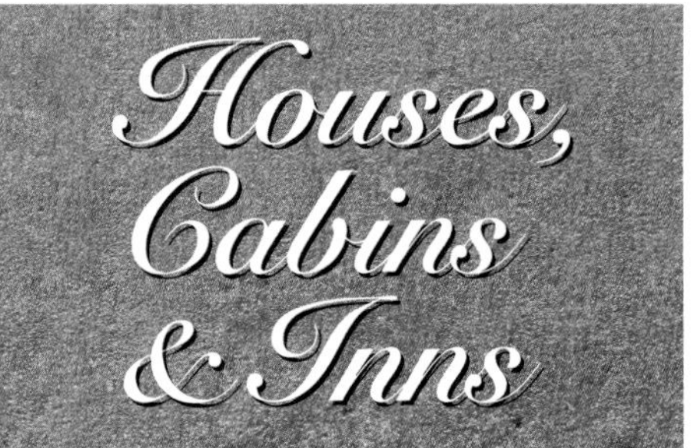

Classic Gingerbread House

DESIGNER: Sally L. Fredrickson

*I*F YOU'RE *a traditionalist, it's hard to beat a design like this one—dripping with sugar and icing and candy decor. The delight is in the details, plus the polished finishing touches, from stencilled designs iced onto windows and the mosaic-like front path of candy fruits to the twinkling gumdrops on the ridges of the roofs.*

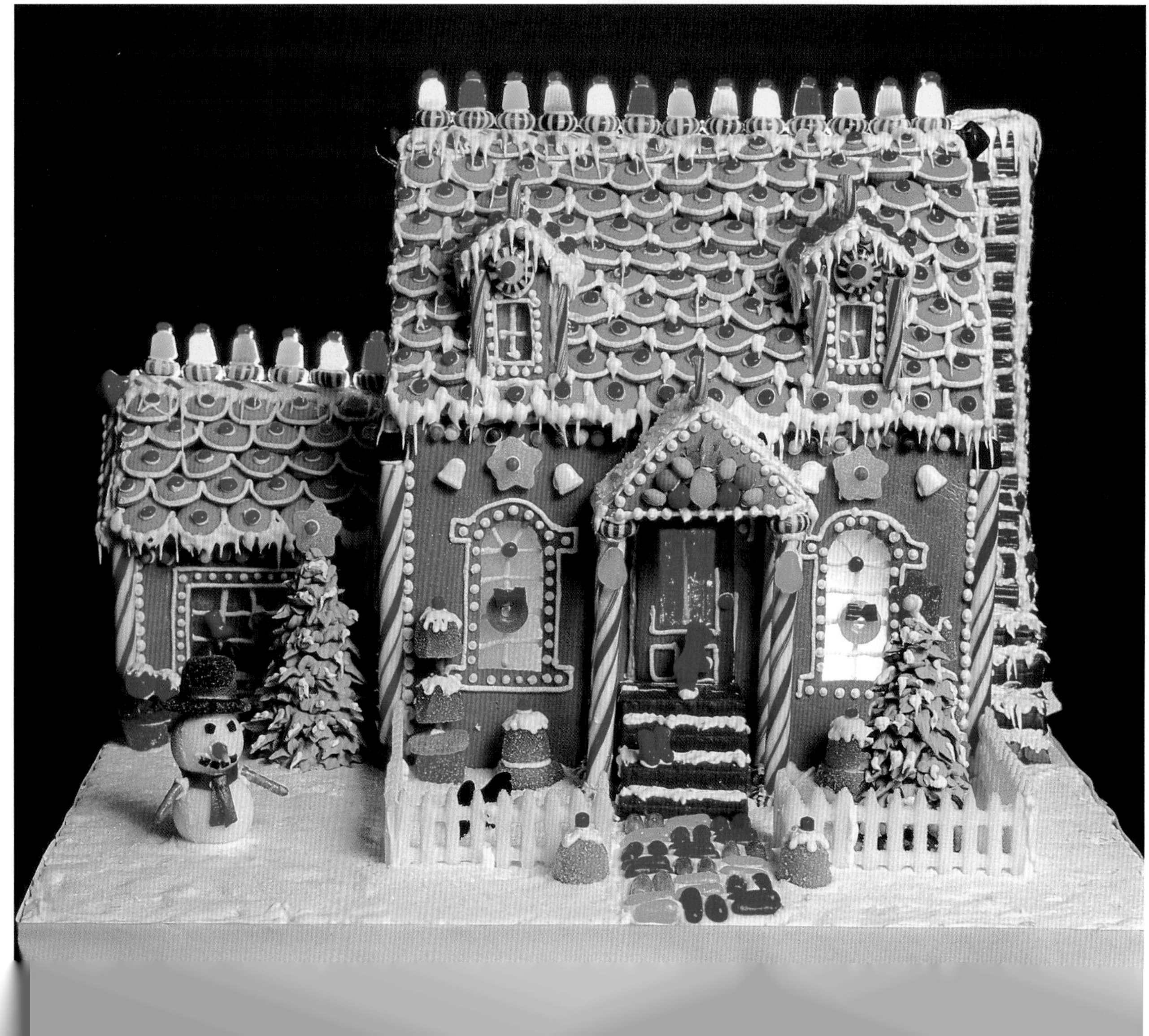

The snowman in the yard sparkles when the light hits him, as if his body is made of real packed snow. The process for making one is simple, and the result is a sturdy decoration. Pack granulated sugar and a few drops of water into tablespoon-size measuring spoons. Let these half balls dry (and harden) into shape, then ice them together for perfectly formed snowballs. Create as many as you need—and build away.

Create a neat little picket fence using a technique similar to the one described above for the snowman. Fence molds are available at shops that carry cake decorating supplies. Pack them with the same sugar-and-water-drop mixture, then immediately dump the molded sugar onto a flat surface covered with wax paper. Your fence pieces should be dry in a couple of hours.

Red licorice pieces mortared into place make a perfectly uniform brick chimney. Tootsie Rolls covered with royal icing snow form an ideal log pile to lean up against it.

A shingling style like this, using layered wafer cookies and accents of Red Hots, takes a little time and a careful eye, but the attention to detail adds loads of charm.

Don't forego the research process (that is, strolling the aisles of candy stores) advises Sally Fredrickson and many other gingerbread house builders. It's the only way to spot licorice dogs, little candy boots, bells, lanterns, and other accents you need to make your gingerbread house a home.

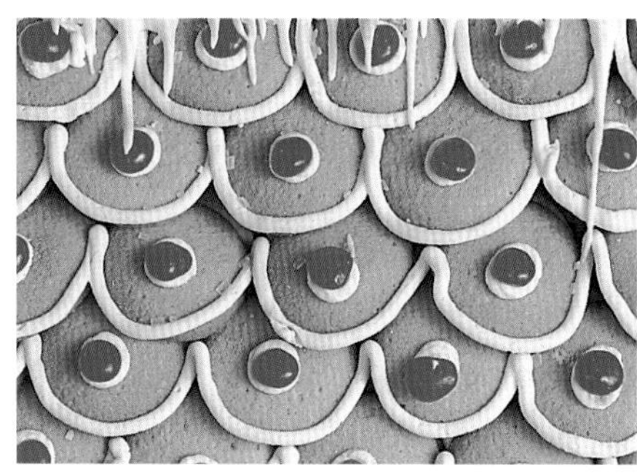

Red Brick Estate

DESIGNER: David Handermann

A HOUSE *covered in candy doesn't have to have a storybook look. David Handermann covered his gingerbread walls with sticks of gum, crafted pillars out of Tootsie Rolls, and formed mortared stone steps from caramels—all resulting in a realistic bit of architecture. The open back, with its dollhouse-style rooms, creates a whole new set of decorating possibilities for bakers who are interior designers at heart.*

If you're leaving out a side wall so viewers can peer into the rooms of your house, be sure to compensate for the support that wall would have provided, especially if you're building a house with multiple levels. Divide the interior space, particularly on lower levels, into several small rooms. The walls in between will make up for much of the missing support.

Hanging curtains, positioning pictures, and setting tables in gingerbread houses is easier if you plan ahead. Remember, once the walls are up, weaving your wrist down a hallway to pipe in a bit of decoration can be tricky (or impossible). Plot out in advance which details and accents you'll need to add before assembling your house. David Handermann even sketched a floor plan to help him decide what would go where and determine how much detail he needed.

French doors add a fancy touch that's especially appropriate on an elegant house like this one. If you're making your own, be sure you have at least 1/2 inch (1.3 cm) of space between the edges of the windows and the outer edges of the doors, or the constructions might be too fragile to resist cracking.

Haunted Halloween House

DESIGNER: Tracy L. Sonia

HERE'S a warning: Once you're hooked on sculpting structures out of gingerbread, you may not stop at Christmas. And if you're straying from icicles and wreaths, there's no better time to stroll the candy aisles searching for supplies than that official celebration of sweets—Halloween.

From gummy worms and candy corn to miniature pumpkins and pre-formed chocolate bats, Halloween is a time when stores are overflowing with ready-made answers to gingerbread decorating dilemmas. There are other times of year, too, when lots of the props you need are packaged up and ready to go, whether you want to try a Valentine's cottage covered with candy cupids and hearts, or an Easter village full of chocolate bunnies and chicks.

For "scary trees" with as much personality as these, cut your tree shapes, faces and all, out of gingerbread dough. (Be sure to cut small mouth and eye holes. They may expand a bit as the trees bake, and if the holes are too large, the expansion could cause the tree to break in half.) In addition, cut two small half circles for each tree. You'll use them, as shown in the photo, as braces on the base of each tree. Once the baked trees have cooled, decorate them as you please, then stand them in royal icing and add the braces.

Over the River and through the Woods

DESIGNER: Sam Marshall

THE young designer of this scene modeled it all after his grandparents' home, which he replicated complete with a side porch and gabled windows. His approach shows how much landscaping can bring a display to life—and it demonstrates that it's okay to mix and match your motifs. Here, the upturned starlight mints lining the pathways provide an enchanting contrast to the realistic coconut-topped evergreens.

Candy Land Christmas

DESIGNERS: June Smith and Shanon Smith

ONE way to come up with a concept for your gingerbread creation is to let the candy be your guide. For a charmingly tidy look, stick with a color scheme (like the bright palette of pastels featured here). You can also allow the shape and style of the candy itself to determine design detail. The fruit candy on this house cries out to form scalloped edges on the roof, and the bright candy bits in the window boxes shape themselves into the most imaginative of flowers.

Lollipops, like the cone-shaped pastel swirls in this display, come in all shapes and sizes, and many of them are a wonderful material for trees. However, if you're entering a contest that tells you all parts of your gingerbread creation must be edible (or if you simply want to pass the edible test yourself), you'll need to remove the suckers' sticks. Pop them in a microwave for just a few seconds to soften them up, then carefully twist them until the sticks pull out.

Want to add a dash of realism to your candyland fantasy? Try licorice root for an authentic-looking wood pile.

Avonlea Inn

DESIGNER: Kristen Cook

DRIPPING *with delicate icicles, draped with strings of garland, and sparkling with candlelight, this elegant inn is the quintessential Christmas house—and it's based on the real thing. With the precision of a budding architect and the artistry of a potential pastry chef, college student Kristen Cook used a turn-of-the-century inn she once visited as the model for her gingerbread masterpiece. Working from a photograph, she replicated the ornate building's balconies, gables, porches, and peaks. Following is the step-by-step process she recommends for creating a gingerbread version of a real-life house of your dreams. Many of the decorating details Kristen used are described in The Trimmings, beginning on page 20.*

FROM REAL LIFE TO GINGERBREAD

1 Start with a photograph of the house. If you have access to the house, take your own photographs, making sure you shoot every side and many angles, so once you start to create templates and later build, you can easily see how the "pieces" fit together. When scouting subjects, Kristen suggests, pay attention to how architecturally challenging they are. If a structure you're interested in has lots of bay windows and complicated rooflines, for example, be sure you give some thought ahead of time to the work involved in recreating those features in gingerbread. The photo on the right shows the image Kristen used as her inspiration.

2 Make a rough sketch of the four sides of your house, mainly to get an idea of how the sizes of various features will relate to one another. This process would help you determine, for example, that you want your bay windows on the front of your house to be half the size of your entrance.

3 After sketching the sides, draw a "footprint" or bird's eye view of your structure. This sketch shows you the various roof pieces you'll need to create to replicate peaks and overhangs. The footprint also gives you an idea of the basic shape of your structure—such as whether it's an L shape or a rectangle—and shows you more about how dimensions relate to each other. Figure 1 is Kristen's footprint.

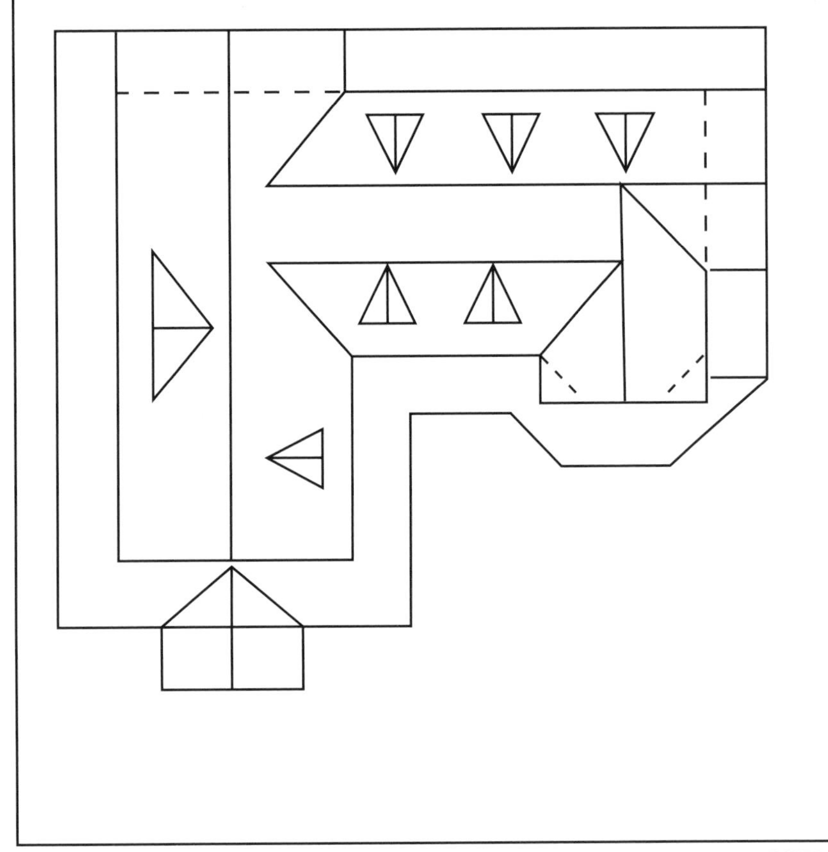

FIGURE 1

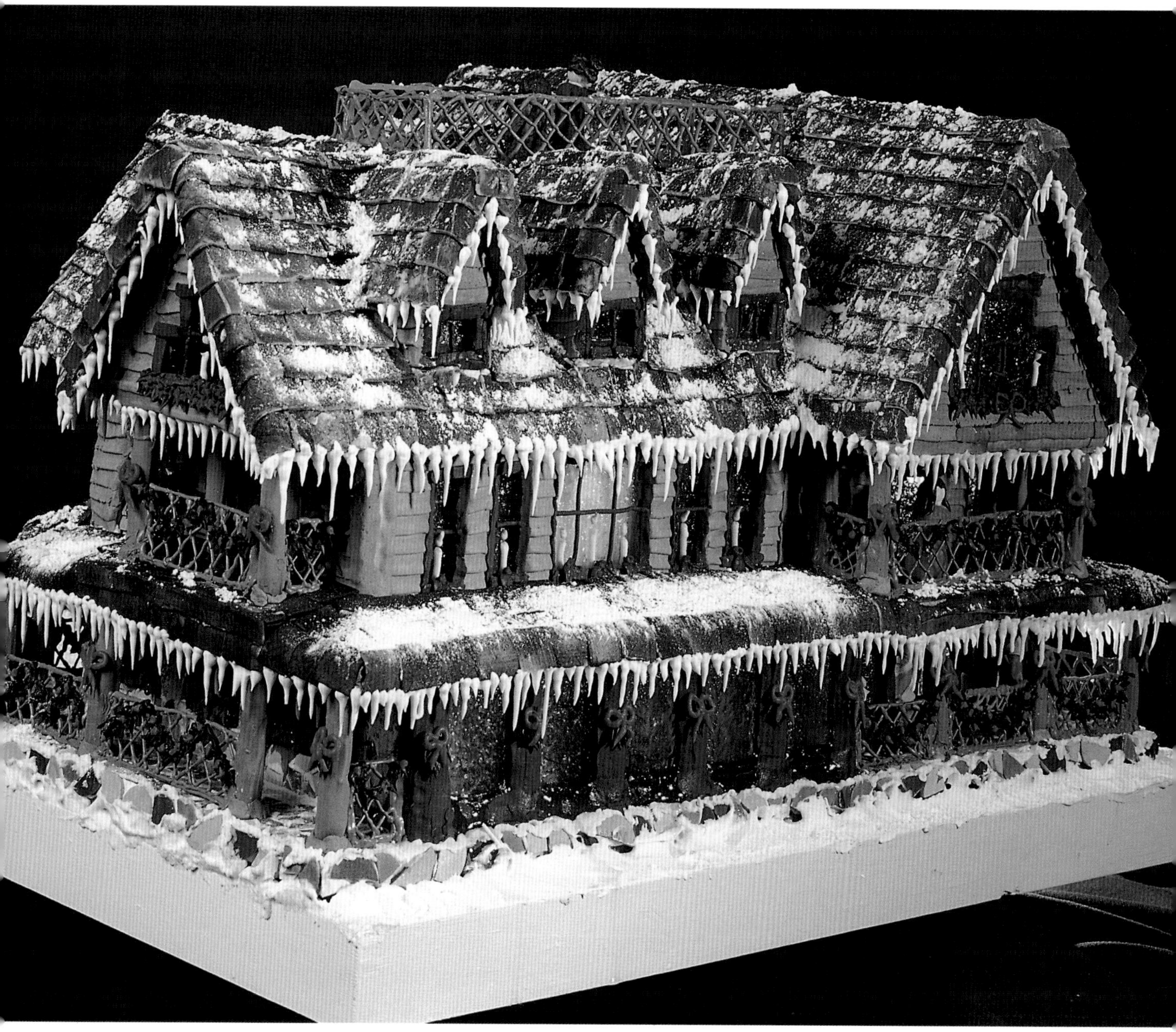

Tip

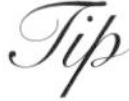

GINGERBREAD is not always consistent. Learn to work with imperfections and make them part of the creative process. **—Kristen Cook**

4 Using your sketches as guides, make an actual-size drawing for each side of your house, detailing each feature according to the size it will be when reproduced in gingerbread. It's best to use an architect's ruler (inexpensive and available at most hardware or office supply stores) for this step. It will allow you to make quick conversions if, for example, you want ¼ inch (.6 cm) on your rough sketches to equal 1 inch (2.5 cm) on your to-scale drawings. When adding windows, doors, and other features at this stage, Kristen says she gets most of her ideas from the actual structure, but also exercises artistic freedom, sometimes adding or subtracting features and changing placement. Figure 2 shows Kristen's drawing for the left side of her inn.

5 From your to-scale drawings, create pattern pieces. Begin by studying one side at a time and determining where you have solid sections that can be single pieces of gingerbread. Once you have pattern pieces for the basic structure of the house, move on to other pieces, such as porches, overhangs, window dormers, and other projections. Measure and cut out doors, windows, and any other openings you plan to create. For details on making pattern pieces, see page 11.

Kristen echoes the advice of nearly every designer featured in this book: Create pattern pieces for your entire house—and make sure they fit together as planned—before you attempt to create your house out of gingerbread. That's especially critical for a structure as detailed as this one. In fact, Kristen baked and assembled the walls of her house first, then experimented with various pattern pieces for her multi-peak roof design before settling on the ones she used.

The trick with a house this intricate is support, support, support. Kristen made double roofs everywhere she could, reproducing the small roof over the entrance and icing it in under all of her larger roofs. Flat areas always need extra support, too, so she added a duplicate layer of gingerbread under her widow's walk and other similar spots.

Figure 2

Gingerbread Genealogy

Gingerbread has been around since early Christian times, when ancient Romans baked it in portable ovens. As early as the 1500s, inventive bakers began using it as a decorative building material. The fragrant pastry became popular in early American cooking because it was inexpensive to make—and because it could survive the unpredictability of wood- and coal-fired ovens.

AVONLEA
INN

Sweetheart Cottage

DESIGNER: Karen Powell

A FEW sentimental (and simple!) touches transform this traditional gingerbread house into a romantic getaway. Use a heart-shaped cookie cutter to create patterns—then turn the pieces you've removed into stepping stones and swinging signs. The twists on this technique (from snowflakes to stars) are as abundant as your collection of cookie cutters.

Bridge and Sign

Cut and bake your gingerbread pieces according to the templates on page 115. When your baked pieces are ready, use royal icing to assemble them according to the following instructions.

1 For the bridge, lay one of the two bridge pieces on its side, with the side you want to be the inner wall of your bridge facing up. Pipe royal icing along the edge of the curved bottom of the bridge, then begin to settle Bit-O-Honey candy pieces on end in the icing. Mortar the candy pieces side by side horizontally to create a "brick" bottom for the bridge (see figure 1). Once the candy pieces are firmly set, attach the second side of the bridge by piping icing along the curved bottom and connecting it to the ends of the candy pieces.

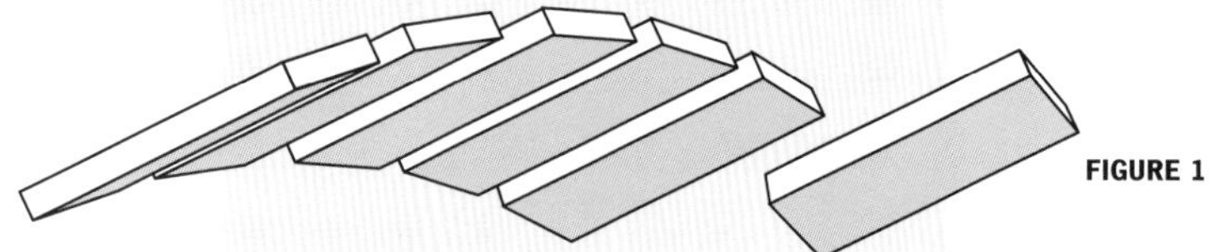

FIGURE 1

2 For the sign, ice the two base pieces together like a sandwich, then settle them upright in a bed of royal icing where you want the sign to stand. Press a thick, sturdy pretzel stick into the icing between the tops of the two bases, cover it with more icing to hold it in place, and let it dry thoroughly. The pretzel stick serves as the rod from which your heart-shaped signs will hang. Attach a heart cookie to each side of the pretzel stick so that they hang back to back. Before hanging them, you may want to decorate the hearts with initials or other lettering or symbols.

Traditional Log Home

DESIGNER: Pam Johnson

*W*HEN *you're building with gingerbread, sometimes it makes sense to draw on the same techniques you'd use if you were constructing the real thing. Pam Johnson borrowed some expertise from her husband (who builds log homes for a living) to create this mountain retreat, using a butt and pass log pattern mortared over a gingerbread frame. Cut your logs out of rolled sheets of gingerbread when the dough is cold, and be sure to use precise measurements if you'll be piecing them together in a pattern. When you mortar them in place, spread the icing on separately for each log; it dries too quickly to allow you to ice a whole panel at once. Use sticks of gum cut into thirds and rubbed with food coloring to create a cedar shake roof.*

Wee Cottage

DESIGNER: James Marshall

*I*T SEEMS *so obvious. Small houses are sometimes better for small hands. Reduce the standard house template (provided on pages 112–114) by 50 percent (omitting the pieces for the porch and chimney additions). You'll be able to bake your four walls and two roof pieces on a single pan. Pull them out of the oven and you've got a child-size house that's manageable to assemble, yet still an ample canvas for creativity. Cutout cookies are perfect for finishing the scene.*

Candy-coated Cottage

DESIGNER: Laurey C. Masterton

*B*ANISH *restraint. Put a muzzle on that little voice that suggests maybe you've gone far enough. If your goal is a classic candy cottage, then "more is more" should be your mantra, says Laurey Masterton. Layer Life Savers on top of gum drops. Ice peppermints over a base of gingerbread people bordered by Skittles. And for a final flourish, top everything with dots of icing festooned with dragées (the small, edible, silver-coated balls available in cake decorating shops).*

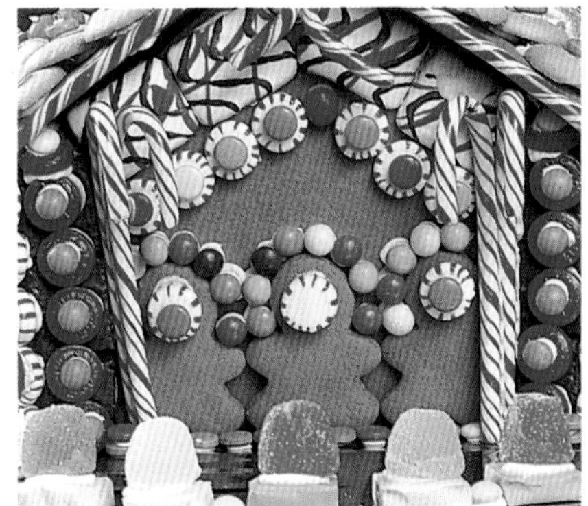

Storing Your Gingerbread House

It's possible to preserve a gingerbread house for several seasons. If you want your masterpiece to last from year to year, consider shellacking it with either food shellac or regular shellac. Then, pad it with plastic (wadded up grocery bags work well) and wrap it in plastic wrap until it's airtight. Store it in a cool, dry spot.

When you unpack your house each holiday season, you may have to do some minor repair work—fixing some chipped icing here or adding a few fresh peppermints there. Displaying your house in a cool, dry spot (away from the fireplace, for example) will help it last longer. And be sure to keep it out of reach of curious—and hungry—pets.

Stonecreek Inn

DESIGNER: Trish McCallister

REAL life is often the best inspiration for gingerbread fantasy. So much so that, in Trish McCallister's case, she has a hard time driving down a house-lined street—and she's in real trouble if she finds herself in an historic district. When an architectural feature catches her eye, she immediately begins imagining how she could recreate it out of gingerbread, icing, and candy. She combined the features of various structures she's noticed over the years to create this cozy, creek-side inn.

Stagecoach

Cut your gingerbread pieces according to the templates on page 121, then bake and assemble them according to the following instructions.

1 Because you'll shape the bottom piece of the stage coach to fit the sides, bake the two side pieces first, and let them cool.

2 Once the side pieces are cool, bake the other pieces. When they come out of the oven, as soon as the bottom piece is cool enough to handle yet still warm and pliable, bend it until it curves to conform to the bottom of the side pieces, and allow it to cool into shape.

3 When all the pieces are cool, ice the sides and the bottom together and allow them to dry. Position the footrest at the front of the coach, the roof on top, and two wheels on each side. Decorate the stagecoach, and fill any open spaces with toys, presents, and passengers.

Templates for the horses also appear on page 121.

Create barren, winter trees like these out of colored pastillage. Roll and shape the trunks and branches separately, let them dry, then assemble them with royal icing. For more details on creating shapes out of pastillage, see page 35.

You can make stone pieces like the ones that cover the facade of this inn out of pastillage or fondant. Myriad other materials can also be used for realistic-looking stones, from brown gourmet jelly beans and walnuts to marzipan and raisins. Simply slather royal icing on the gingerbread, then "mortar" your material in place.

Tip

IF you're building a house for a competition or for some other purpose that requires strict attention to detail, you may not want young helpers joining in the fun on *your* house. In that case, be sure to have materials available for kids to make their own houses (perhaps with graham crackers). Our children were upset that they couldn't help with ours until we got them started on their own. **—Hobey Ford**

Gingerbread Times Two

DESIGNERS:

Students enrolled in the Culinary Technology Program at Southwestern Community College under Program Coordinator Ceretta Davis

IF BUILDING *one gingerbread house is fun, think what a good time it will be standing two side by side. You could use this duplex design to make people see double, like the builders did in this case. Or, if you can't decide on your decorating approach, here's your chance to try a couple. Maybe one side houses the city slickers and the other side is home to their country cousins—or one is a tribute to candy and icing while the other is a realistic turn-of-the-century brownstone.*

Mountain Hideaway

DESIGNER: Bill Bena

Toss precision out the window if you're after the rustic look of rough-hewn timbers. Vary shape and thickness as you roll your logs, then texturize their surfaces with a knife. For a glossy finish, brush them before baking with a wash of egg mixed with milk or water (just be aware that this might slightly deter your gingerbread from hardening as much as it would without it). Finally, enhance the homespun look by painting your color detail directly onto the gingerbread, using a paint-brush dipped in food coloring.

Candlelit Cottage

DESIGNER: Kathy Moshman

MAKING a gingerbread house is like getting a new dollhouse every year. I try to create houses that make people want to go inside. **—Trish McCallister**

*T*HERE'S *more than one way to make your gingerbread house glow. Using color flow (described in detail on page 24) can produce shiny, bright windows like the ones on this cozy cottage. Once the windows are completely dry, you can pipe candles and other decorations on their surface. You can use the same technique for scalloped roof pieces over your windows, or you can fashion them out of pastillage or gingerbread.*

Snow-covered Cottage

DESIGNERS:
Phillip, Vickie, Noah, and Lindsey Capps

THIS sweet design variation has storybook appeal. It's as simple as a standard, box-shaped house, but the cottage's charming angles and open facade inspire decorations of whimsy and fantasy. For the Capps family, the design also inspired snow—plenty of it—complete with snowbound revelers making the most of a recent storm.

Cottage

Cut and bake your gingerbread pieces according to the templates on page 120. When your baked pieces are ready, use royal icing to assemble them just as you would the house in the Gingerbread Baking and Building Basics section.

Pretzel Cabin

Designer: Julia Marshall

ICING *thick pretzel sticks on top of a gingerbread base is a quick way for kids (and bigger builders on tight schedules) to transform a standard house into a log cabin in the country. If you want a clever way to play with indoor decor, leave the back side open, and fill your rooms with candy figures. Color coconut green for leafy-looking trees like these, and melt blue hard candies for a pond.*

Castles, Chapels, Villages & More

Coventry Alley

DESIGNER: Alex Russell

*F*LIPPING *the traditional gingerbread layout shifts everyone's focus. Those who feast their eyes on this display can take a visual walk down a turn-of-the-century lane and into the heart of the hamlet. Placing the buildings on the perimeter leaves you with lots of shop window space inside to fill with everything from baskets of fresh-baked bread (peanuts are the perfect thing for these little loaves) to fruit roll up curtains and tiny hats of piped icing.*

If your project is heavy on architectural detail, consider creating two sets of templates. That way, you can leave the model you create for your trial run intact, and use your other set for cutting out your gingerbread pieces. When it's time to assemble the real thing, the model serves as a great guide.

Dried spaghetti creates the effect of window panes without obscuring the view of the scenery you fussed over inside.

Don't be afraid to leave well enough alone if you're creating a display with this much detail. Alex Russell, for example, said he made everything from street lamps to benches to add to his village setting, but decided not to use them because they blocked visitors' views of all the goodies inside his shops.

Tip

PLAN the size of your project so that it's something you can reasonably complete—with time and energy leftover for adding lots of details. **—Alex Russell**

Sweet Shopp

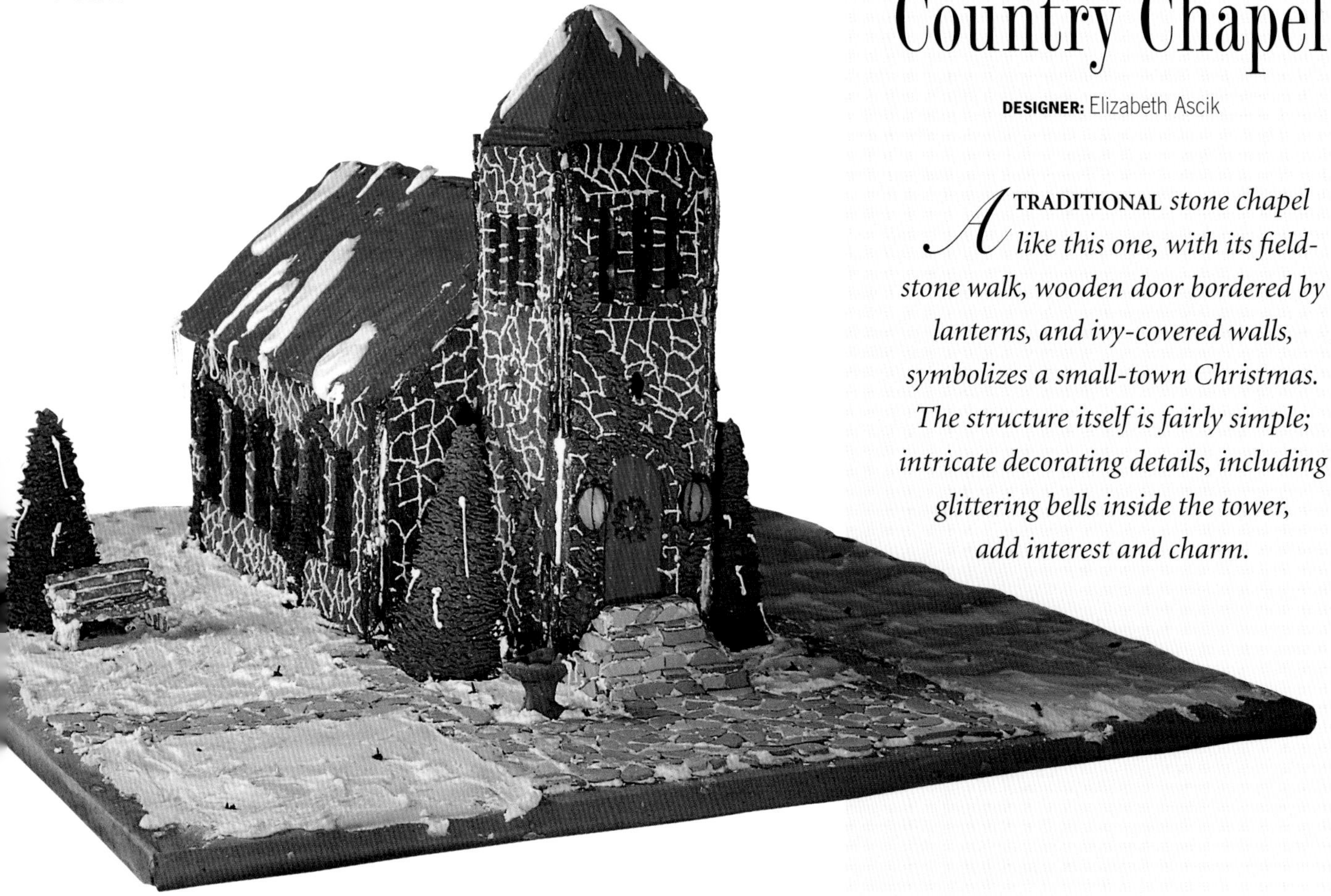

Country Chapel

DESIGNER: Elizabeth Ascik

A **TRADITIONAL** *stone chapel like this one, with its field-stone walk, wooden door bordered by lanterns, and ivy-covered walls, symbolizes a small-town Christmas. The structure itself is fairly simple; intricate decorating details, including glittering bells inside the tower, add interest and charm.*

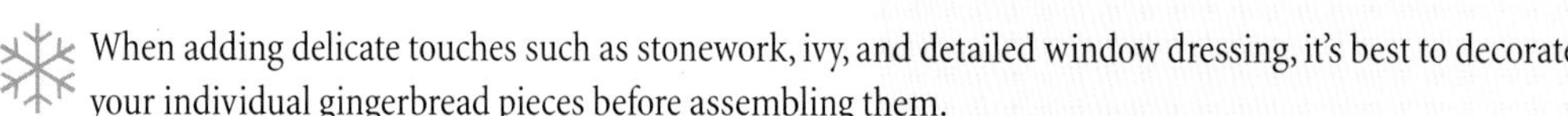

When adding delicate touches such as stonework, ivy, and detailed window dressing, it's best to decorate your individual gingerbread pieces before assembling them.

These stone walls are an inventive variation on the usual technique of icing stone-like material onto gingerbread walls. For this more aged look, use a knife tip to cut tiny ridges into your gingerbread before baking it. After it's out of the oven, use a thin icing tip to fill the ridges with "mortar."

Simple effects can add loads of character. Thin grooves made with a knife in the roof's red icing, for example, create the look of a tin roof. Tufts of grass peeking through the snow and tiny footprints near the path (a Barbie doll is the perfect tool for this) finish off the scene.

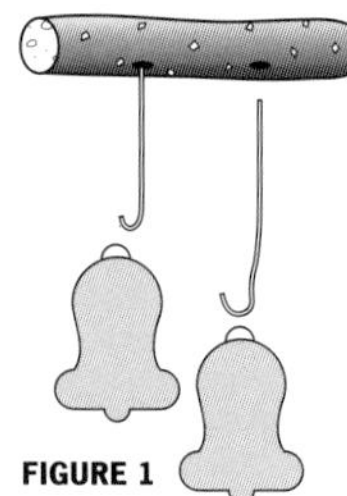

FIGURE 1

If you want to keep all the materials that adorn your house edible (that is, after all, the fun—and the challenge—of making a gingerbread house), there are times when you'll have to view food as hardware. Hanging inside this church's tower, for example, are two tiny, glittering bells engineered into place with a clever collection of food products. To make your own, create two molded chocolate bells with brackets made of angel hair pasta that has been cooked, molded, and dried into shape. Mold more pasta into the shape of hooks, and use these to suspend the bells from holes poked into a pretzel stick rod (icing the ends of the hooks into the rod). Brush the finished bells with gold luster dust before hanging them in place. Figure 1 shows how the bells and hanging apparatus fit together.

Sugar Cube Castle

DESIGNER: Tymber Lewis Lance

THERE are several ways to stray from the classic gingerbread base when you're constructing out of candy. Using sugar cubes like building blocks is one of the easiest—and it's a familiar technique for young first-timers. Spread some royal icing on your base and plunk down the perimeter of your structure with a single layer of sugar cubes, then mortar more layers (like bricks), one on top of the other. Try upside-down ice cream cones to form turrets if you want a castle like this, and use thinned-out royal icing colored green to pipe alligators in your moat.

VARIATION

Sugar Cube Lighthouse

DESIGNER: Drew Rowland

Christmas by the Sea

DESIGNER: Linda Hafler

WHY stop with a single structure? Pick a central theme, add all the architecture that logically belongs, and you end up with an entire settlement of sweets. Linda Hafler focused as much on the accompanying buildings (including a boat house, fog bell house, fuel house, and keeper's living quarters) as she did on her lighthouse. The result: a full seaside setting dressed with details ranging from docked boats and sandy shores to marsh grass.

Lighthouse

1 To make a round, tapered lighthouse like this one, start with a foundation of Rice Krispie treats. Bake approximately three batches, then stuff the gooey, greasy matter into a large, tapered, plastic beverage container (the kind you might use for a gallon [3.8 liters] of iced tea or lemonade). Pack the Rice Krispie treats firmly, and let them sit for several hours; then turn the container over and slide out the formed structure (which is greasy thanks to the butter and marshmallows in the mix).

2 Place your tower (situated where you want it in your display) in a bed of royal icing, and let it sit for another several hours. (If you want your lighthouse even taller, bake more Rice Krispie treats and pack them into a similar beverage container that is several sizes smaller, then ice the addition to the top of your first tower.)

3 To finish the top, bake two circular pieces of gingerbread (approximately 6 inches [15 cm] in diameter). Ice one to the top of the tower, and add a large yellow gumdrop in the center for the lighthouse lamp. Arrange gingerbread cutout shapes in a circular fashion around the edge of the bottom circle, then place the second circle on top of these. For additional ornamentation, you can create intricate shapes from royal icing and attach them to the rim of the second circle.

4 Finish off the structure with an upside-down gingerbread cupcake decorated with icing, then cover the tower with a flat layer of royal icing to resemble plaster. You can use colored royal icing for windows and jelly beans for bricks.

Create boats like these from chocolate fondant (available in prepared form at cake decorating shops). The sand dollars can be shaped out of white fondant, and the starfish can be made from white fondant marbled with pink and peach food coloring paste. Don't blend the colors completely; the color variations add to the realistic look. Dried macaroni shells are perfect for filling out your coastline.

Shredded wheat cereal is just the thing for dried tufts of marsh grass popping up out of the snow. Break the cereal apart, pluck a few long strands, and prop them upright in royal icing.

Use white fondant just as you would clay to piece together a snowman like this one. You can color bits of the fondant to add accents of ear muffs, buttons, a scarf, and a nose. Try chocolate string licorice for skate blades and the ear muff band, and poppy seeds for eyes.

Christmas at the Corner of Town

DESIGNER: Bridget Brochu

CHOOSE a community theme that combines several sites, and you can add even more of the details that bring a display to life. Make windows with different shapes of cookie cutters, then use clear gelatin sheets (available at cake decorating shops) for glass—or simply leave them open so people can see what's inside. Accent your church interior with pews and an altar (Bridget created hers out of graham crackers and licorice), and fill the café with tables, chairs, and even tiny plates of food.

Scottish Castle

DESIGNER: Elizabeth M. Prioli

THIS shimmering fortress makes a spectacular impression, partly because of its collection of regal towers and turrets, and partly because of its realistic detail—right down to the wood grain on the castle doors. You can achieve some of the same effects using standard cake decorating supplies and a key prop from the hardware store.

Shops that stock cake decorating supplies carry molds you can use to make impressions on rolled-out sheets of gingerbread dough. You'll be able to find molds that press in patterns of rustic stonework like you see on these castle walls, as well as molds to texturize the surface of pieces you want to represent wood. For flat walls, use the molds on your dough, then cut the dough into the house shapes you need.

If you've got a roasting spit accessory in your oven (or can rig one up) and a hardware store nearby, you can create tall, skinny turrets just like the dazzling array you see here. Purchase electrical conduit pipe in several different diameters. For each turret, cover a piece of pipe with parchment paper held in place with masking tape, grease the paper, then roll a piece of gingerbread around it tightly (using the pipe as you would a rolling pin) until the dough adheres to the paper. If you want to texturize the surface of the dough, use your mold at this point. You should also cut out any windows or other openings (a craft knife works well for cutting tiny window slits like the ones shown here). Slip the pipe on the roasting spit and begin baking, turning the pipe about every eight minutes, so the dough bakes evenly and doesn't sag on one side. When it's completely cool, your turret should slip right off the pipe. If you don't have a spit accessory, try resting your dough-covered pipe on chopsticks so your baking piece won't completely flatten on one side.

For the fantasy effect of frosty white color, start with a lighter variation of gingerbread baked with corn syrup instead of molasses. Next, sponge white liquid food coloring over your baked pieces. Once you've achieved the lightness you want, brush off any standing liquid, then brush the pieces with cornstarch to help dry them out. You may even want to pop them back in the oven again. Finally, use a paintbrush to apply petal dust (a cake decorating ingredient used in sugar-craft flowers) and another to sprinkle the pieces with silvery luster dust (also found in cake decorating shops). Two caveats to keep in mind if you want to work toward this stunning look: The process is time consuming, and the addition of liquid food coloring can soften your gingerbread. If you want your house to stand solid for a lengthy holiday showing, you might want to skip the liquid whitening technique.

Large boulders for your castle grounds are easy to form out of lumps of gingerbread. As they bake, their shapes become even more amorphous; then they can be painted with liquid food coloring.

When stacking sections (like the turrets of multiple heights shown here), an internal superstructure of support is critical. Elizabeth Prioli used stacked rice cakes (perfect because they're dry, contain no oil, and can be sawed into shape) cemented together with royal icing. She filled unsupported internal areas with stacks approximately 8 inches (20 cm) high, wedged bread or pretzel sticks in at every joint, then topped everything off with a piece of baked gingerbread.

Sweet Shop & Florist

EASY to imagine Charles Dickens himself strolling past this picturesque corner of a quaint village street. Judy Searcy combined two of her favorite art forms—baking and flower arranging—to come up with her concept. Then she set about developing it in delightful detail.

DESIGNER: Judy E. Searcy

To make rounded display cases like those that characterize these shops, cut a large coffee can in half (top to bottom), cover the rounded surfaces with greased parchment paper, and lay the dough strips that will form the rounded cases on top of the cans for baking. The baked display cases then attach to wide openings on the standard square buildings behind. Make sure you cut the front openings on the buildings to match the height and width of the coffee can you're using for your display window molds, or you'll risk having noticeable gaps where they meet. After the baked windows have cooled, use their curved outline to create a template for shelves that will fit inside. The shelves will probably have to be whittled back into shape a bit after baking. Then they can be glued into place with royal icing.

For the awnings above the display cases, bake gingerbread molds in the rounded surface of a cake ball pan (available at cake decorating stores), then cover them with rolled fondant.

The darker, aged look of the gingerbread helps add an old-world quality to these shops. To achieve the effect, bake your gingerbread very slowly for several hours, removing it every hour or so to brush it with egg whites. Let it cool before putting it back in the oven.

In some cases, you may also want to apply color each time you remove the baking gingerbread from the oven. To give her clock tower a wood-grain color and texture, for example, Judy mixed brown food coloring paste with a small amount of egg whites, applied it with a fine artist's brush, used a dry brush to smear in wood-grain lines, then continued baking the pieces until she was happy with the color. She used a similar technique for the brick on the back of the bakery, first scoring the surface with the tip of a seam ripper, then applying a mixture of red and brown food coloring paste and egg whites with a wide, soft-bristled pastry brush. When applying color in this way, color and bake all the pieces that are to be the same shade at the same time, otherwise the tints are likely to vary. Also, it's easier to add color than to take it away, so brush it on and bake it in several stages until you achieve the shade you want.

Swing around back, and you get a view of what's happening behind the scenes at these corner stores. They're filled with floral bouquets, wedding cakes, and even a Hobart oven. Judy made miniature versions of popular pastries using marzipan as a base, then adding decorations with royal icing, a very small writing tip, and "a steady hand." The flowers were formed from icing and fondant with stems of uncooked angel hair pasta and vases of poured sugar shaped over tiny molds. Seeds and nuts add texture to the arrangements.

For basic information on creating decorations and details from fondant, marzipan, and other confections, see pages 30–32.

Feliz Navidades

DESIGNER: Emily Grace Young

FORGET the North Pole. Emily Grace Young let her imagination drift southward (southwest, to be exact) to come up with this holiday hacienda and church. She also used a clever gingerbread alternative that's perfect for younger builders—graham crackers. You can glue them together with royal icing, just as you would pieces of gingerbread. If you want to cut out windows and doors, do that first by warming the crackers briefly in the oven to soften them up. Because graham cracker structures are quicker and easier to assemble than walls and roofs of gingerbread, they leave small chefs plenty of time and energy for decorating. Use pink-tinted royal icing to create adobe-like surfaces, and accent your buildings and yard with easy-to-find foods. The wagon here features pretzels and pasta wheels. Sugar wafer cookies form the well and the cactus. And a sprinkling of brown sugar gives a sandy sparkle to the warm-weather holiday scene.

Tree House with a Twist

DESIGNER: Anthony Pelle

*I*N THIS *twist on a traditional tree house, the structure grows right out of the tree trunk itself, then it's topped off with limbs poking out of the ceiling. Though the design is an imaginative variation on the basic house theme, this is a simple starter project for a young, first-time builder. It's compact, too; all of the pieces fit in a single 12- x 18-inch (30 x 45 cm) pan.*

Cut and bake your gingerbread pieces according to the templates on page 115. When your baked pieces are ready, use royal icing to assemble them according to the following instructions.

1 Assemble the tree trunk first by standing the eight trunk pieces and the trunk door piece in a circle, connecting each piece with icing.

2 Add the round base on top of the trunk, and allow the structure to dry thoroughly.

3 On top of the round base, assemble the house pieces just as you would a standard house. In the holes on one side of the roof, insert gingerbread tree limbs and secure them with icing.

Hendersonville Depot

DESIGNERS: Steven, David, and Suzanne Uhlman

MAKING a baked replica of a local landmark is a popular way to personalize your gingerbread creation. The Uhlman siblings chose their town's train depot as their subject. They started with a photo of the structure, then brainstormed how they would pull it off in gingerbread. The basic rectangular building is simple enough, but the challenge, they found, was fashioning and inserting the hexagonal clock tower jutting through the depot's roof. The instructions below tell you how to do it.

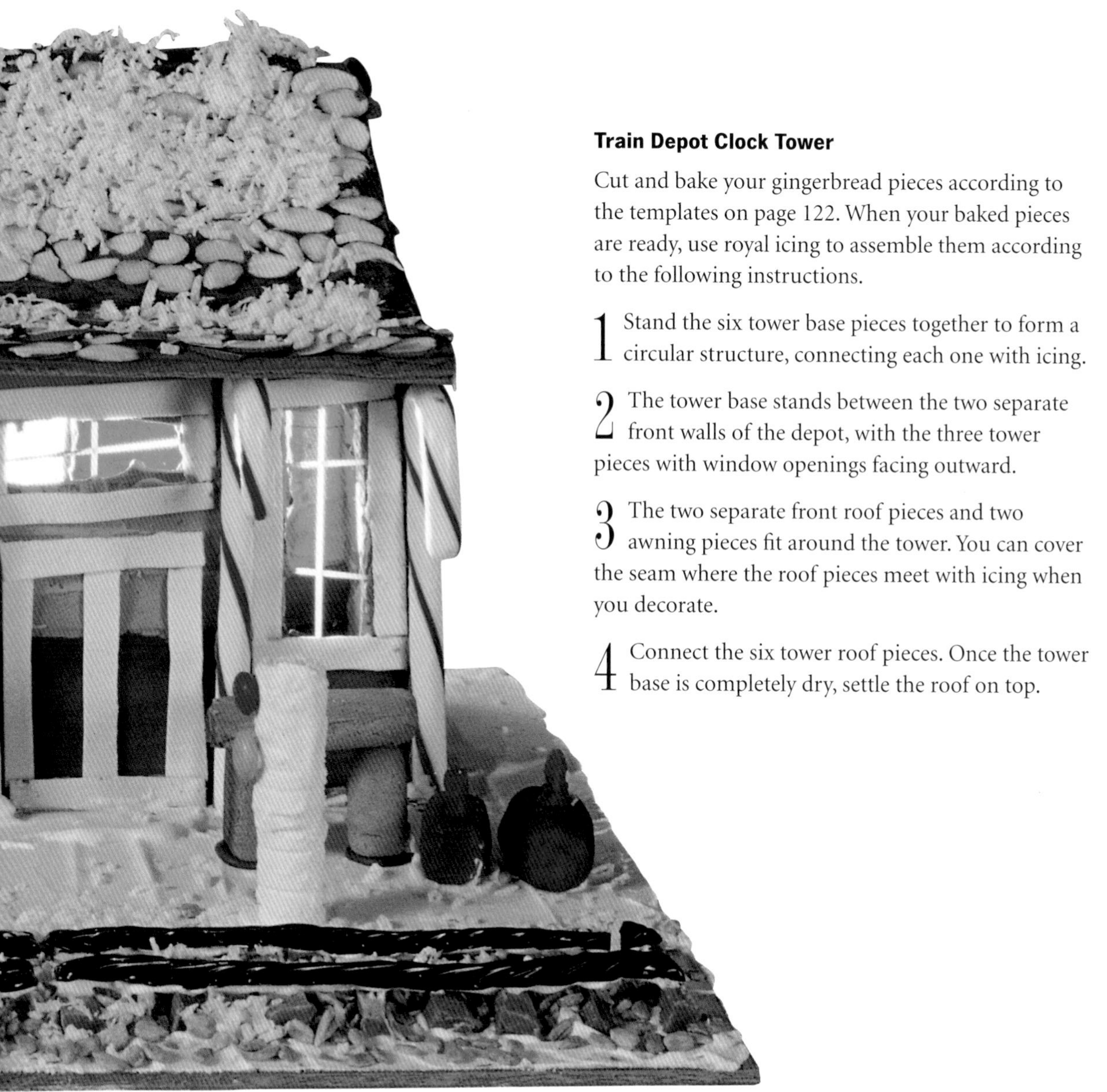

Train Depot Clock Tower

Cut and bake your gingerbread pieces according to the templates on page 122. When your baked pieces are ready, use royal icing to assemble them according to the following instructions.

1 Stand the six tower base pieces together to form a circular structure, connecting each one with icing.

2 The tower base stands between the two separate front walls of the depot, with the three tower pieces with window openings facing outward.

3 The two separate front roof pieces and two awning pieces fit around the tower. You can cover the seam where the roof pieces meet with icing when you decorate.

4 Connect the six tower roof pieces. Once the tower base is completely dry, settle the roof on top.

Little Red Schoolhouse

DESIGNER: Karen Graham

*N*ATURAL-LOOKING *shades of red and brown give this schoolyard scene its charm. The secret is in brushing the color onto your gingerbread pieces when they're still in dough form, then baking it in. Possibilities abound for adding all the people and props to make an appropriate playground. Karen Graham used marzipan to craft most of her additions (including the scary snake), then finished off her display with a dusting of powdered-sugar snow. We've provided tips on the coloring process and a template for the school bus.*

Coloring the Schoolhouse and Bus

1 For the schoolhouse, add several drops of red liquid food coloring to a paper cup of water. Use a pastry brush to apply the colored water to the surface of your dough shapes. Be sure not to add too much, or the water will run off the sides of the dough and cause the baked gingerbread to curl on the ends (creating problems when you attempt to line up pieces evenly). The coloring process will likely give your unbaked dough a pinkish appearance, but don't despair. Baking will deepen the color, creating the darker brick shade you're looking for.

2 To darken the roof of the schoolhouse, beat two or three eggs, then brush them onto the unbaked roof pieces. Again, be careful not to add too much liquid; you simply want to cover the dough. As the egg glaze bakes in, the pieces will develop a dark, glossy appearance.

3 You can give your school bus its traditional orange hue by mixing liquid orange food coloring and water (just as you did for the red color in step one, above), then painting it on the unbaked dough shape with a small paintbrush. For added detail, don't color the window areas orange; instead, paint them with a mixture of brown food coloring and water. A template for an easy school bus appears on page 118. Once you're ready to decorate, add small, white breath mints for headlights and round candy for wheels.

The More the Merrier

Gingerbread houses make ideal projects for organizations ranging from youth groups to scout troops. Brenda Rogers, who teaches home economics at Chapman High School in Inman, SC, helps more than 60 students each year prepare for gingerbread house competitions. Topping her annual shopping list is 200 pounds of sugar, which her students transform, along with the other ingredients, into churches, barns, lighthouses, filling stations, and modern homes with swimming pools. "They love the idea that they can make something they've always seen but had no idea they could create themselves," she says.

Zookeeper's Paradise

DESIGNERS: Anna and Todd Olsen

THERE are places for creatures that creep, crawl, swim, and soar in this whimsical animal village, complete with aviary, reptile house, penguin pond, and more. The architecture offers more variety and a bit less challenge than a traditional gingerbread house—and the approach leaves lots of room for creativity when it comes to filling the fenced-in areas with your own menagerie. All of that makes it the perfect project for an adult-child team, say the mother-son duo who created this version. Flip back to the building and landscaping ideas beginning on page 27 for tips on fences, rocks, water, and other fun features you can use in your own zoo. Instructions for making the display's three structures are provided here.

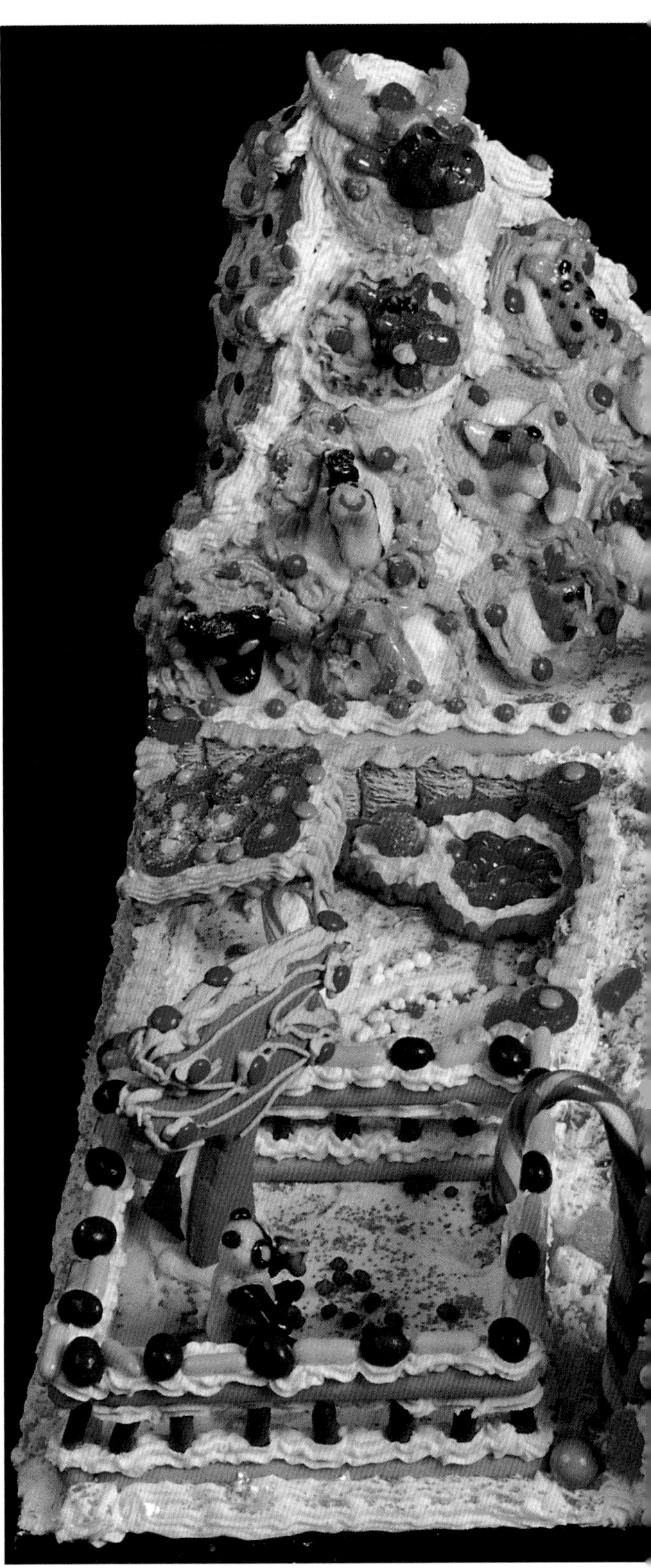

THINKING about what would be fun and interesting to do with my houses each year is what I really enjoy. I get as much pleasure out of the planning as I do from actually creating them. **—Elizabeth M. Prioli**

Tower With Animal Faces

This clever tower of ice cream cones is easy to build—and even more fun to decorate with an array of furry faces peeking out.

1 Stack 11 small ice cream cones on their sides in a pyramid, fixing each row in place and adding bulk to the structure by icing mini marshmallows between the gaps. Use five cones on the bottom row, three on the next one, two on the third row, and one on the top.

2 Cover the structure with icing and decorate it as desired.

3 Attach a wreath around each ice cream cone opening, and stick a large marshmallow into each. Attach different animal face (the ones shown here were made of marzipan) to each marshmallow so that the animals appear to be poking their heads out of windows in the tower.

For instructions on making wreaths, see page 25; for instructions on crafting figures from marzipan, see page 30.

Aviary and Reptile House

Cut and bake your gingerbread pieces according to the templates on page 123. When your baked pieces are ready, use royal icing to assemble them according to the following instructions.

1 Trim the windows of the circular aviary with icing and candy, then add as many feathered friends as you like inside before attaching the roof. An edible ice cream cone dish (available most places ice cream cones are sold) turned upside down is perfect for topping off this structure. The one shown here is decorated with a layer of pretzel sticks for a thatched hut look.

2 Assemble the walls of the reptile house just as you would the walls of a traditional house. (The right side wall has an opening for an alligator to swim out into an attached pool.) After you've filled the reptile house with your creeping creatures of choice, the roof fits like an awning across the back.

Cathedral at Christmas

DESIGNERS: Thomas Marshall and Jamie Merritt

*C*REATE *a regal house of worship with a two-story facade and elegant arched windows, all adorned with minimal, classic touches. For frosty, amber-colored windows like these, cook poured sugar until it caramelizes.*

Totem Pole Lodge

DESIGNER: Tenley Rae Alaimo

*I*T'S HARD *to imagine a more adventurous example of the fact that gingerbread is not just for candy Christmas cottages anymore. With tinted fondant passing for birch bark, licorice straps standing in for leather ties, and slivered almonds imitating chopped wooden accents, Tenley Rae Alaimo breaks with tradition in bright, bold style. You can build this most basic of box-shaped houses by adapting the standard house design illustrated on pages 112–114. Creating the scene is all decorating fun—adding totems and other touches in the most vivid colors and candies you can get your hands on.*

- Use fondant (see page 35) to make strips of birch bark for decorating your base. For appealing variation, color several different batches of fondant, creating bark ranging in shade from tan to deep brown. Then roll pieces of fondant out by hand until you have thin strips to work with (or run your fondant through a pasta machine, which makes this process even easier). If you want the crude look of natural bark, resist the temptation to use a knife to even up all the edges of your rolled fondant.

- Before icing them into place, use a craft drill with a small bit to create holes in the fondant pieces where you plan to run straps of licorice. Attach the fondant to the base, allow it to dry until it's secure, then whipstitch the licorice into place.

- A wide, flat roof like this one can sag if it isn't supported well from inside. One easy and effective way to provide that support is to buy a loaf of inexpensive white bread and allow it to sit out for several days, until it takes on rock-hard form. You can then whittle the stale bread into the shapes you need and stack the pieces like a thick deck of cards inside your structure, gluing each layer together with royal icing.

A SINGLE, *distinctive feature can set your gingerbread display apart—and provide the inspiration for even more decoration and detail. In this case, a colorful covered bridge brings the surrounding millstream setting to life. It crosses a stretch of poured sugar water, complete with rock candy river rocks.*

Covered Bridge Mill

DESIGNERS:
Derek Aldridge, Marquis Brooks, Kelly Tobin

Covered Bridge

Cut and bake your gingerbread pieces according to the templates on page 117. To color your gingerbread before baking it, add several drops of liquid food coloring to a paper cup of water. Use a pastry brush to apply the colored water to the dough. Be sure not to add too much, or the water will run off the sides of the dough and cause the baked gingerbread to curl on the ends (creating problems when you attempt to line up pieces evenly). As your dough bakes, the color will deepen.

When your baked pieces are ready, use royal icing to assemble them according to the following instructions.

1 Start with one of the side pieces of the bridge. Pipe icing along the bottom edge, then place it on the edge of the bridge floor. Hold it in place several seconds until the icing begins to harden. You can also prop it in place with a temporary support.

2 Once the first side is stable, add the back piece, the second side, and the front piece, allowing each to stabilize before moving on to the next.

3 Allow the structure to dry completely before adding the roof pieces.

Firehouse Christmas

DESIGNER: Trish McCallister

I F YOU'VE *got to work on Christmas, might as well make your surroundings merry. So goes the thinking of former nurse Trish McCallister, who has, like the firefighters in her Hook and Ladder 67, spent many a holiday on the job. She pulled ideas for her intricate details from history books, then created an open design to show them off. Use her tips and the template for her fire wagon if you want to try something similar.*

The toughest part of creating a structure like this is building in support pieces, then disguising them, since nearly everything is in full view. Trish used stacks of sugar cubes inside, decorating them so they resembled brick columns. She also stresses the importance of using a neat, clean technique when piping icing along the house seamlines inside.

Think through which parts of your structure you may need to decorate before assembly (tiny details on inside walls, especially, fall into this category). Once you've put everything together, there will probably be areas you can no longer reach with an icing bag.

The template for horses on page 121 can be used to create horses to be housed in the bottom of the firehouse.

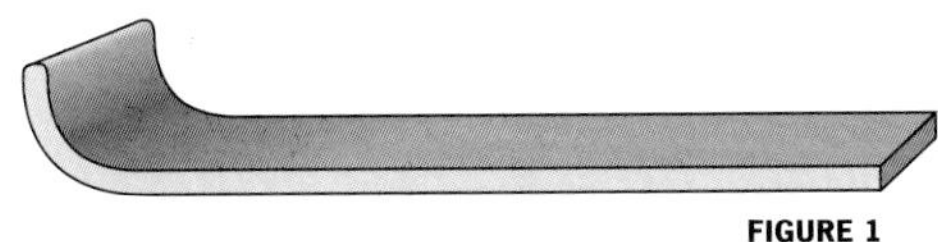
FIGURE 1

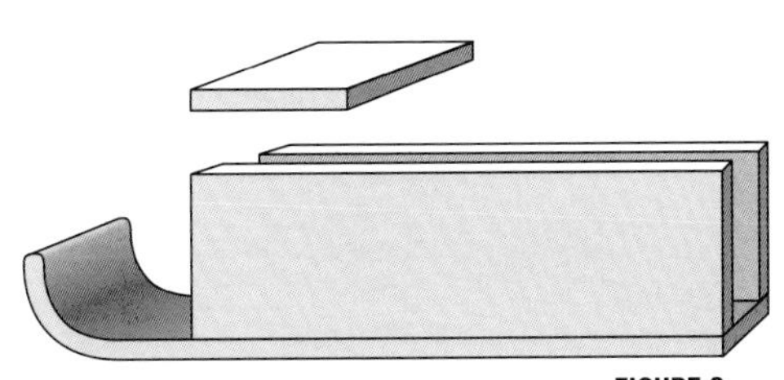
FIGURE 2

Fire Wagon

Cut and bake your gingerbread pieces according to the templates on page 118. When your baked pieces are ready, use royal icing to assemble them according to the following instructions.

1 As soon as you take the bottom piece out of the oven, place it along the side of the baking sheet to form a curve in the gingerbread. As it cools, it will hold its shape (see figure 1).

2 Attach the two sides to the bottom and the driver's seat across the side pieces, just ahead of the curve (see figure 2). Allow this portion of the wagon to dry thoroughly.

3 Add the four wheels, and find something to rest the wagon on overnight to allow the wheels to dry in place.

4 Attach the harness pieces to the front, and decorate the wagon with a water barrel (an ice cream cone makes an ideal base for this), ladders, and other details.

Damsel in Distress

DESIGNERS:
Hobey Ford, Lauren Ford, and Debra Roberts

Here's a fanciful gingerbread creation featuring a fairy tale in progress. (When we enter the scene, the damsel trapped in the castle is being visited by the friendly dragon who has fallen in love with her.) The baking and building techniques Hobey and Lauren Ford and Debra Roberts used are as inventive as the whimsical scene they came up with. They've shared some of their secrets here.

Castle Tower

1 Use aluminum flashing (which you can purchase at a hardware store) to make the castle's main tower. Cut two pieces, each approximately 12 inches wide by 24 inches tall (30 by 60 cm).

2 Form a cylinder with one piece, securing it by wrapping a piece of thin, high-gauge wire (also available at hardware stores) around it and twisting it in place.

3 Form a second cylinder with the other piece of flashing, but make this one approximately 2 inches (5 cm) smaller in diameter. It will sit inside the larger cylinder, and your gingerbread will be baked in the space between the two. This second cylinder, which will have to be removed once the gingerbread is baked, is held in place differently. Use an awl to start a hole in the flashing (from the inside of the cylinder outward), where the edges overlap. Hold the cylinder in place with one hand. With the other, use a short screwdriver to start a metal machine screw through the holes. Screw it tight enough to hold the cylinder in place, but not so tightly that you can't easily remove it later (see figure 1).

4 With leftover flashing, make approximately four clips to hold the cylinders in position. (As the gingerbread bakes, it expands and can push them out of place.) Cut strips approximately ¾ inch (1.9 cm) wide and 3 inches (7.5 cm) long, then bend them into U-shaped clips and affix them evenly around the bottom of the two cylinders (see figure 2).

5 Pre-assemble the cylinders to make sure they fit together as planned. Once you're happy with the setup, take the sheets apart, spray them with cooking spray, then put them back together. Spray a cookie sheet as well, set the cylinders in place on the cookie sheet, and pour gingerbread dough into the slot between the two cylinders until it reaches a level of approximately 10 inches (25 cm).

6 You'll probably need to remove all of the racks from your oven for molds of this height to fit. Simply set the cookie sheet holding the cylinders on the bottom of the oven between the heating elements. You could also set a couple of bricks on the bottom of the oven and place your cookie sheet on top of them.

7 You will likely need to allow more baking time than you would for a thinner, flat piece of gingerbread. Once you're satisfied that your gingerbread is thoroughly baked, remove it from the oven and let it cool for at least an hour. Loosen the screw on the smaller, inside cylinder and very carefully spring it inward by tightening the diameter, then lift it out. Untwist the wire holding the outer cylinder in place and remove it, and you should be left with a 1-inch-thick (2.5 cm) gingerbread cylinder. Now, while the gingerbread is still slightly moist, is the best time to even the top of the cylinder so that it's absolutely flat (a hack saw blade works well for this) and to cut out a window in the tower, if you want one.

8 Bake a circular piece of gingerbread approximately 12 inches (30 cm) in diameter to sit on top of the cylinder. To create the notched top of the tower, fashion a short set of cylinders out of flashing, bake a gingerbread cylinder approximately 2 inches (5 cm) tall, and cut the design out of the top edge with a hack saw while the gingerbread is still warm. The smaller cylinder sits on top of the circular piece of gingerbread.

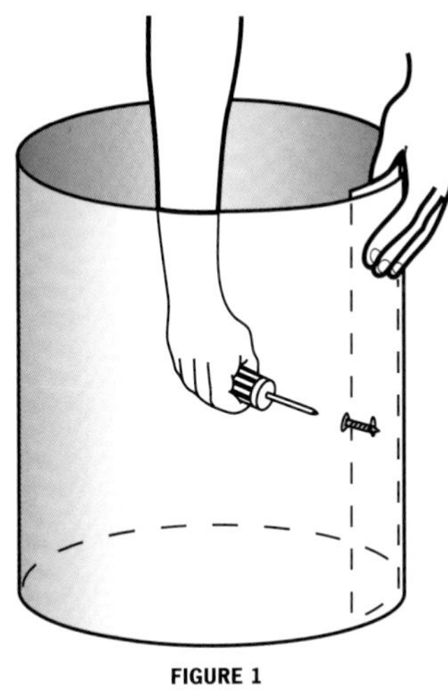

FIGURE 1

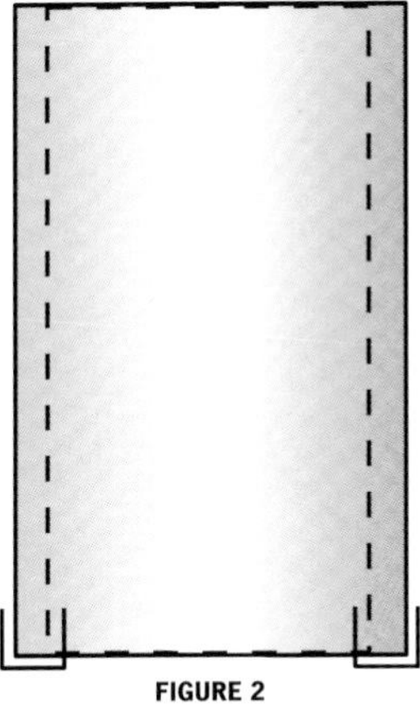

FIGURE 2

Outer Walls

1 Use flashing, again, to create rectangular forms for the castle's outer walls. You can bend the notched shapes into the forms and bake them in.

2 Cut out space in the wall forms for the windows. Then, create small, cookie-cutter-style forms (with a 1-inch [2.5 cm] rim) for the window shapes, and insert them in your wall forms. To hold the window forms together, make small slits on each end, where the flashing overlaps (see figure 3). The window forms can be removed after the gingerbread is baked and used as molds for melting candy for the windows.

Dragon

The best part about a dragon like this one is that he makes failed attempts at other structures (and the resulting broken pieces) worthwhile. (Save all your mistakes.) His body is the glued-together collection of gingerbread scraps salvaged from the rest of your work. If you're in the unfortunate position of having no mishaps to draw on, you might actually have to bake a few random pieces of gingerbread to use for scraps.

1 Start with a fairly sizable "backbone" piece. Use generous amounts of royal icing tinted green to glue chunks and crumbles to the backbone, working toward a general dragon shape. When you come to the tail, legs, and head, you may want to shape some pieces of dough specifically for these features and bake them.

2 When you reach the neck area, build slowly, letting each layer dry and set before adding more.

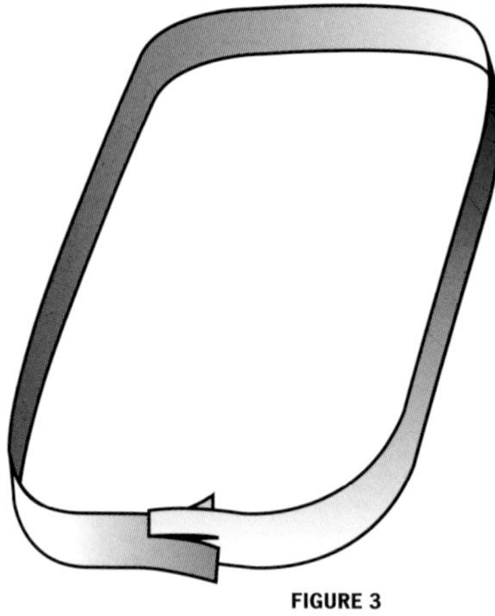

FIGURE 3

3 Once you're satisfied with the shape you've molded, add gingerbread triangles for spines down the dragon's back, then use a curved, crescent-shaped tip and green icing to create scales all over, starting from the bottom and working up.

ADD some turrets and flags to the top of your roof, cover everything in a frosty coat of white, and there's no doubt about it—you've combined the essential ingredients for a palace way up north. Complete the magical scene with a gingerbread cookie Santa and his sleigh out front, attaching the lead deer to a nearby tree to make them look as if they're ready to "dash away all."

Santa's Palace

DESIGNER: Melissa Lance

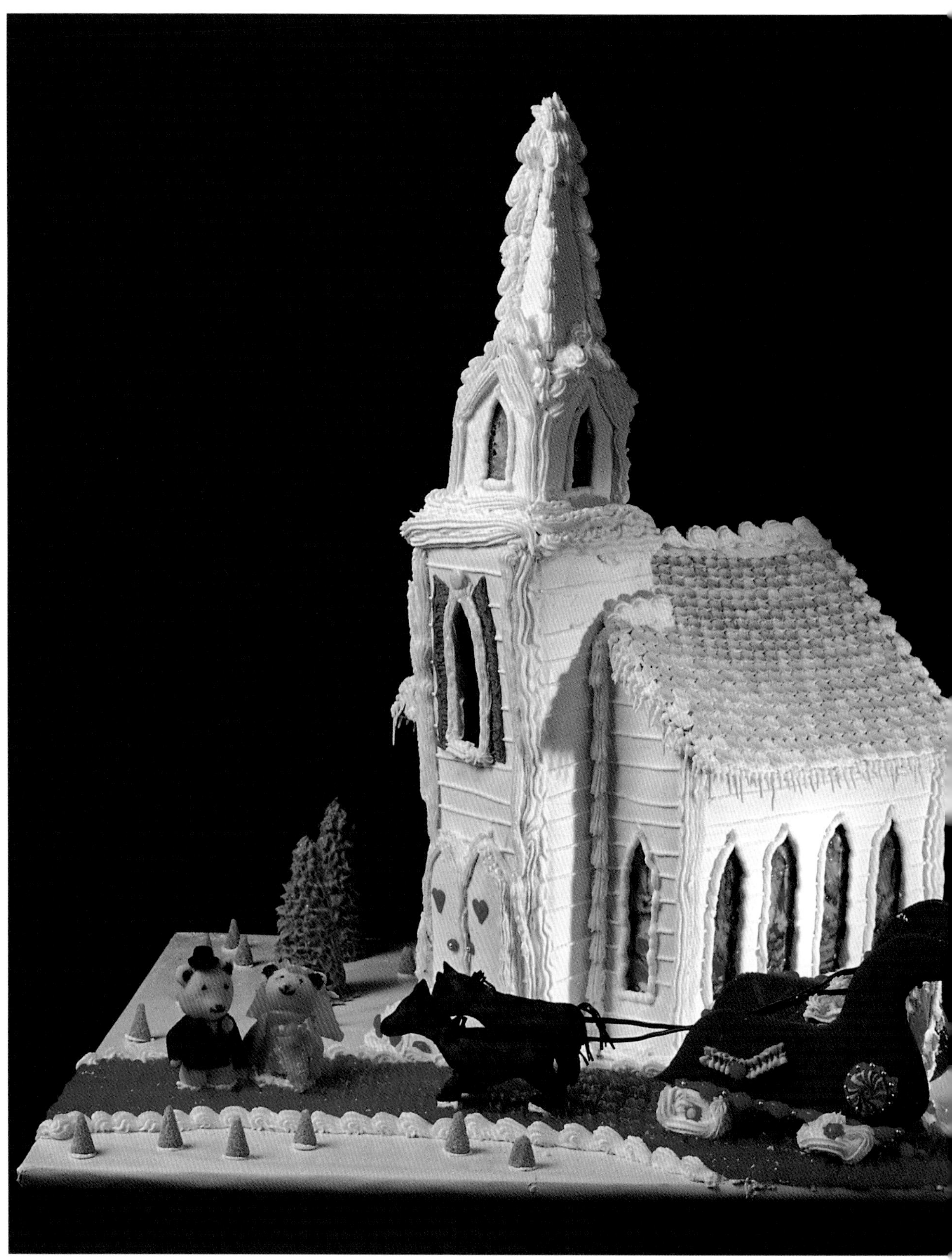

Christmas Wedding Chapel

DESIGNER: Lisa Goelz

CHRISTMAS is for lovers, according to Lisa Goelz, who studded her chapel doors with candy hearts and landscaped the lawn with a bride, a groom, and a just-married sleigh, ready to whisk the happy couple down a red licorice drive. We've provided templates and instructions for the front tower and steeple, which you could adapt to any church structure. Plus, we've included a pattern for the sleigh—a classic feature of many a gingerbread display.

Tower and Steeple

Cut and bake your gingerbread pieces according to the templates on page 116. You'll need to use a serrated knife to trim the edges of your baked pieces if they expand or alter while baking. For your structure to fit together neatly, it's important that multiple pieces made from the same template (all of your A pieces, for example) match in size and shape. When your baked pieces are ready, use royal icing to assemble them according to the following instructions.

1 Connect your four A pieces in a tall, thin, square formation, just like the four walls of a house. (Note that you should have cut out two doors and one window on the front A piece.)

2 Attach piece B like a flat lid on top of the A structure. Let the icing on this structure dry completely before adding additional levels, otherwise your entire steeple might sag or collapse.

3 Connect the four C pieces just as you did the A pieces. Once assembled, the C structure should sit squarely on top of piece B. Let this added structure dry completely.

4 The two D pieces form a peak over two of the opposing C pieces (see figure 1).

5 The E pieces work in pairs, with each pair forming a tiny roof peak over the two remaining C-piece points (see figure 2).

6 Connect the four F pieces along the longest sides to form a pyramid. This steeple point sits atop the roofs created by the D and E pieces (see figure 3).

Don't fret about gaps in the seams of your assembled structure; you can disguise them easily with icing.

Sleigh

Cut and bake your pieces according to the templates on page 117. Then, assembly is simple.

1 The floor of the sleigh fits lengthwise between the two sides.

2 Attach the front and back pieces, in slightly from the ends of the sleigh.

3 Finally, in between the two pieces, ice the sleigh's seat.

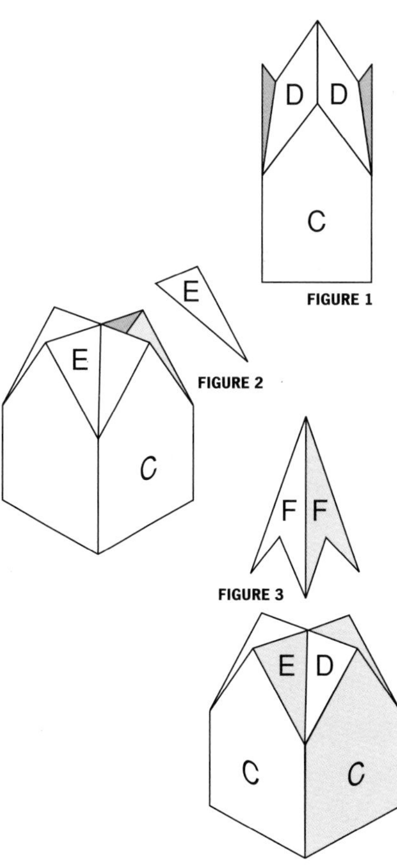

FIGURE 1

FIGURE 2

FIGURE 3

WHAT do you get when you replace candy canes and gumdrops with herbs and spices? In the case of this gristmill, a more rustic and realistic look. Eleanor Berry started with a basic house structure, then added inventive touches—from a hibernating bear in a mountain cave to tiny sacks of meal—to bring her country mill to life.

Down by the Old Mill Stream

DESIGNER: Eleanor Berry

To easily create a clapboard appearance, score the gingerbread that forms the walls of your structure with the long edge of a ruler when the pieces are hot from the oven.

Use hamburger buns as the base for a rocky mound like the one in this display. Dry them out first in a microwave oven (which makes them less fragile than drying them in a conventional oven). Then cover them with gray-colored icing.

For sturdy trees like these, here's an easy, dome-shaped base you can make. Drape a round sheet of gingerbread dough over an oven-safe measuring cup (or any other similar form). Use a straw to press a hole in the top (where you'll later insert a pretzel-stick trunk), then bake it until it's completely dry. After it's baked, use a file to carefully whittle the hole larger, if necessary, sand the bottom of the pretzel stick you're using for a trunk so it will sit flat, and use icing to fix it firmly in the base. Cover the base in a layer of grass-colored icing, and blend it into your setting.

Scattering dried basil, parsley, and red pepper flakes makes believable fallen leaves, and poppy seeds pressed into icing create great gravel.

To build a water wheel like this one, cut and bake your gingerbread pieces according to the template on page 119. In addition, cut two strips of dough approximately 8 inches (20 cm) long and 2 inches (5 cm) wide (or as wide as the crackers or other material you'll be using for paddles). Bake these two strips over the rounded bottom of a stainless steel bowl. Use the two strips to connect your two wheel pieces (see figure 1). Add cracker paddles, angled in every inch (2.5 cm) or so. Finally, use a piece of candy (horehound is shown here) as a washer in the center hole you poked in the wheel. You may need to shave some additional gingerbread out of the hole so your candy will fit.

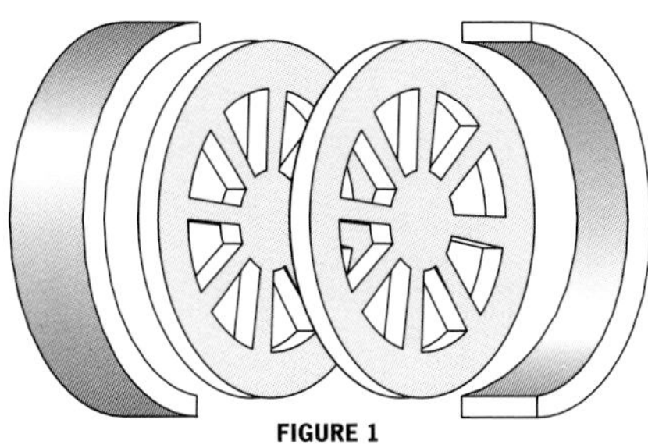

FIGURE 1

Rolling down the River

DESIGNER: Margaret M. Bradshaw

MAYBE you prefer a holiday house that floats. This three-tiered riverboat is fairly basic, just be sure to support the stacked floors on the inside with bread sticks, extra pieces of gingerbread, or some similar material. Coax the pieces that form the bottom two levels into gentle curves by baking them around wads of aluminum foil. Add a staircase up the side of your assembled structure and a stern wheel in the back. Once your boat is floating on a river of blue icing, a sea of decorating possibilities opens up, from a snowy scene on a nearby bank, like the one here, to Christmas-ball buoys and strings of garland circling the decks.

Staircase

1 Cut and bake two sets of risers, using figure 1 as a guide. Determine the height according to the amount of space you need to cover when angling your staircase from the bottom deck to the one above.

2 The width of your staircase should match the width of your decks. Ice small pieces of chewing gum, cut into thirds, into place as treads.

Stern Wheel

1 Start with two circles of baked gingerbread, then flatten the bottoms on each so they'll rest on your icing river, giving the illusion of being partially covered with water (see figure 2).

2 Cut notches around the edges of each circle, and use sticks of chewing gum as slats to connect the two sides of the wheel (see figure 3).

3 Attach the wheel to the boat with a candy cane on each side (see figure 4).

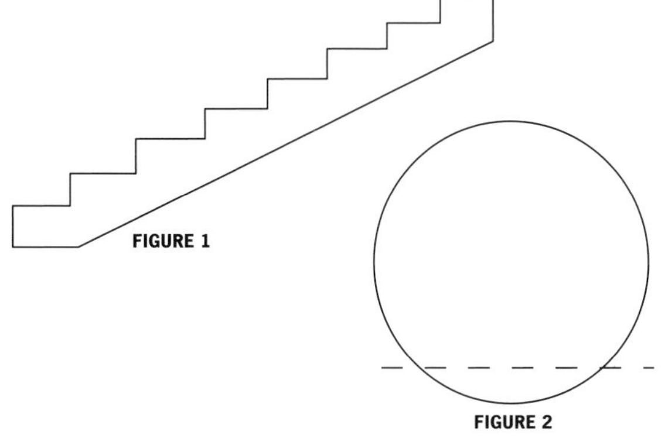

FIGURE 1

FIGURE 2

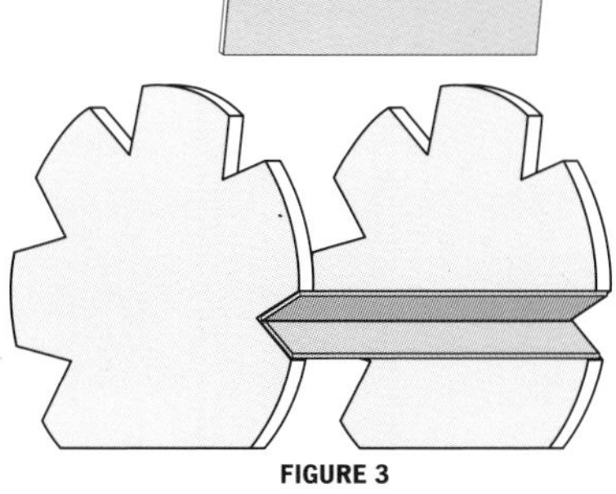

FIGURE 3

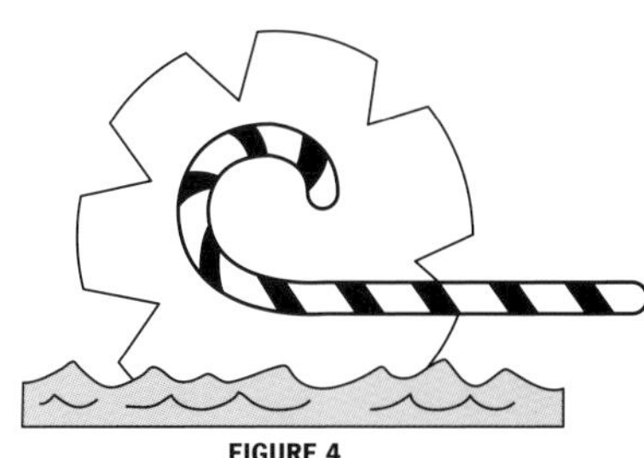

FIGURE 4

Bird's Eye View Estates

DESIGNER: Catherine Gonzales

*W*HO *says gingerbread houses can only be inhabited by make-believe humans? This one's for the birds. The bi-level roost—complete with customized perches, tiny egg-filled nests, and the luxury of an indoor birdbath—shows how fun it is to let your imagination soar.*

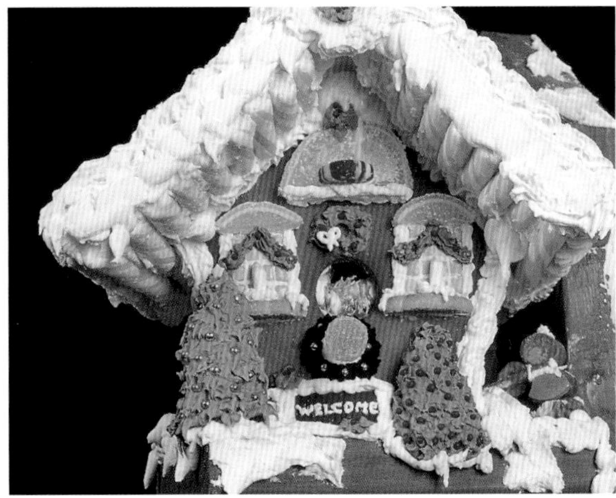

- When you come up with a theme this clever, there's no end to the fun of running with it, whether you're creating scenes inside window openings or signs for the yard.

- If you're working with a space this tiny, it's far easier to add interior decorations (such as the miniature bath towels, soap, and brush shown here) before fully assembling your structure.

GROCERY
Milk

Holiday Village

DESIGNER: Trish McCallister

TALK about a light bulb going off. Trish McCallister started by making a simple chocolate lamppost, just to get the creative juices flowing. Before she knew it, this entire snow-swept village began springing up around her little light. A collection of constructions makes for a striking gingerbread display. Keep your shapes fairly standard, like the ones shown here. Then add your variety in the form of roofing material, window dressing, door shapes and styles, and color. Trish says her plan was to "make people want to look at all the little spaces," as if they were actually touring a gingerbread village. Following are instructions for the lamppost she started with. If you're searching for an idea, making one of these might have an illuminating effect on you, too.

Lamppost

Pipe chocolate pieces according to the templates on page 119, then assemble them according to the following instructions, using piped chocolate just as you would royal icing for your "glue." You could also make the lamp out of royal icing.

1 Run a bead of chocolate around the perimeter of the small square. Position the four side pieces one at a time, holding each piece until the chocolate you've set it in begins to harden (see figure 1).

2 Pipe a small candle out of white and yellow royal icing, allow it to harden, and set it in a dot of chocolate or icing inside the lamp.

3 Run a bead of chocolate around the top rim of the side pieces and attach the large square (see figure 2).

4 Attach the lamp to the post and the post to the round base. Add a dot of chocolate to the top of the lamp for accent.

Work in a cool place when making your lamp, since chocolate is susceptible to heat.

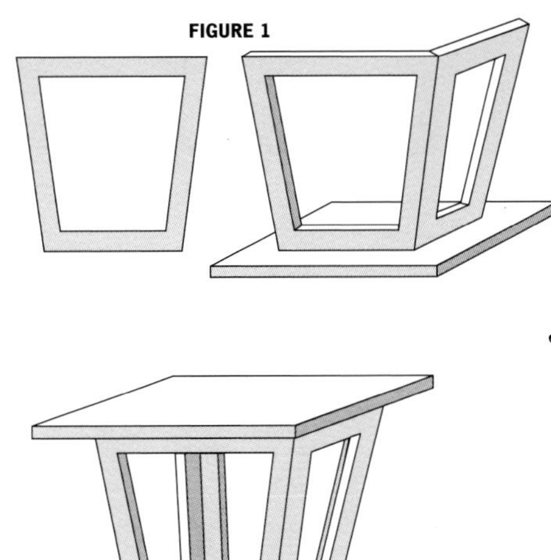

FIGURE 1

FIGURE 2

Tip

When creating a display of multiple structures, it's especially important to use exact measurements and be precise when cutting your gingerbread so everything fits together well.

*M*ERRY *is definitely the word. This festive carousel is a snap to bake and assemble. Use all your leftover good cheer to create bright-colored frosting for carousel paint, then decorate your horses for a Christmas carnival. You can adapt the horse template on page 121. Cookie cutters come in myriad animal shapes, too, if you want to add a few more figures to the celebration.*

Merry-Go-Round

DESIGNERS: Misti Henderson and Melissa Kirk

Lighthouse Landing

DESIGNERS: Katra Johnson and Ginger Smith

LONG to escape to sand and surf come mid-December? Use the fantasy as your muse and whip up a gingerbread lighthouse situated on a lapping shore. For white-washed walls that look as if they've spent some time in salt air and bright sun, use a soft, natural-bristle brush to add white food coloring powder to your baked gingerbread.

Tip

A PLASTIC scraper is an excellent tool to have around when you're making a gingerbread house or, more to the point, when you're cleaning up the kitchen counter. **—Hobey Ford**

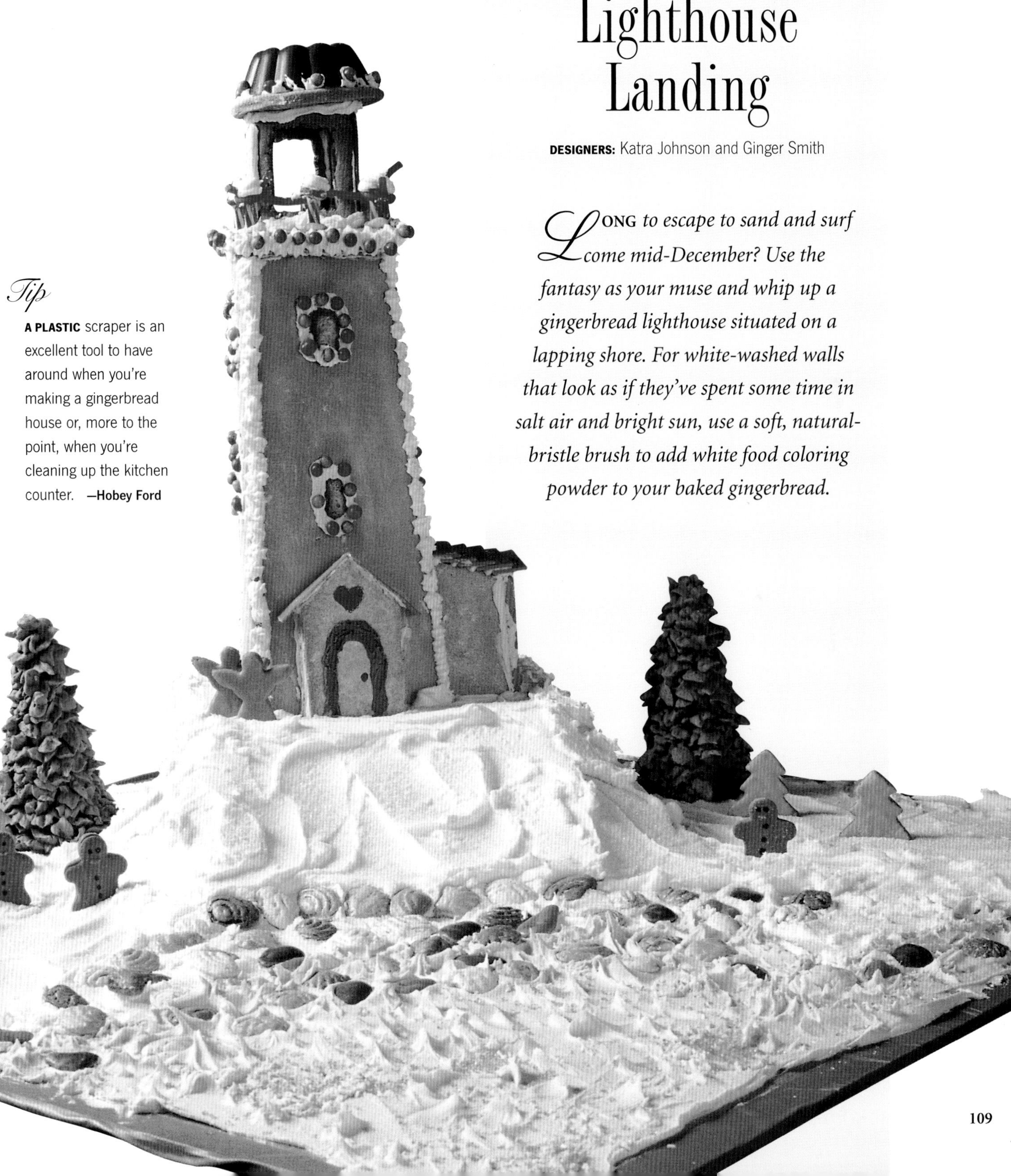

Ladies and Gentlemen: Start Your Ovens!

GINGERBREAD is not just for recreational bakers anymore; it's been raised to competition status. Entering gingerbread house contests—with their promise of cash, prizes, and widespread recognition—is becoming a wouldn't-miss-it holiday tradition for many.

The historic Grove Park Inn in Asheville, North Carolina, hosts one of the largest and best-known competitions in the United States. More than 100 entrants from across the country, ranging from kindergartners to grandparents, fill a wing of the inn with everything from gingerbread barns and chalets to haciendas and arks. Since 1993, participants have been attracted to the renowned competition, with its team of judges from across the country, by awards of cash, accommodation packages, and commemorative plaques for all. In recent years, some have also been lured by the promise of fame—the competition's edible works of art have been featured on "Good Morning America," CNN, and the TV Food Network, and in the pages of *Southern Living, USA Today*, and more.

One of more than 40 trees that provide the backdrop for *A Grove Park Inn Christmas*.

Gingerbread houses on display on "Gingerbread Lane," a main attraction at *A Grove Park Inn Christmas*.

Entering the competition puts participants at the center of the Grove Park Inn's six-week holiday celebration, *A Grove Park Inn Christmas*, which transforms the legendary turn-of-the-century mountain resort into an elegant Christmas village. From late November through New Year's Day, garlands, wreaths, poinsettias, and more than 40 decorated Christmas trees provide the backdrop for animal nature displays, an elves' playhouse, and the sleeping quarters for Major Bear (he's the inn's beloved holiday ambassador who makes appearances daily).

Guests can have their photo taken with Santa, participate in candlelight caroling in the Great Hall, take a guided historic walking tour, or sing along with the Grove Park Inn staff chorus beneath a 25-foot Christmas tree. To keep visitors fueled for all the festivities, the award-winning inn offers special holiday buffets daily, where classic dishes include roasted turkey, apple-sage dressing, mandarin-cranberry relish, and homemade Christmas stollen.

The Grove Park Inn Gingerbread House Competition is open to both amateurs and professionals. Prizes, awarded in an adult division and two youth divisions, are based on the following criteria.

1. Overall appearance 2. Originality/creativity 3. Difficulty 4. Precision 5. Consistency of theme

For details, an entry blank, and information on the Grove Park Inn's free gingerbread house workshop, call 800-438-0050, ext. 8045, or write to Grove Park Inn, 290 Macon Ave., Asheville, NC 28804.

TEMPLATES

Most of the following templates for gingerbread structures and accessories are too large to appear full size, so they've been reduced by 50 percent (which means you'll need to enlarge them to 200 percent on a copy machine to create structures or accessories exactly like the ones shown in the book). A few of the templates have been reduced even more. We've provided specific instructions on each template that requires enlarging.

The simplest way to transfer a template to cardboard (or whatever pattern material you've chosen) is to copy the template on a copy machine (enlarging it if necessary), cut it out, then use the cut-out paper copy as a guide to trace the design onto the cardboard. Finally, cut out your cardboard pattern using scissors or a craft knife, and label each piece clearly.

Basic House

PIECES SHOWN AT 50%—ENLARGE 200%

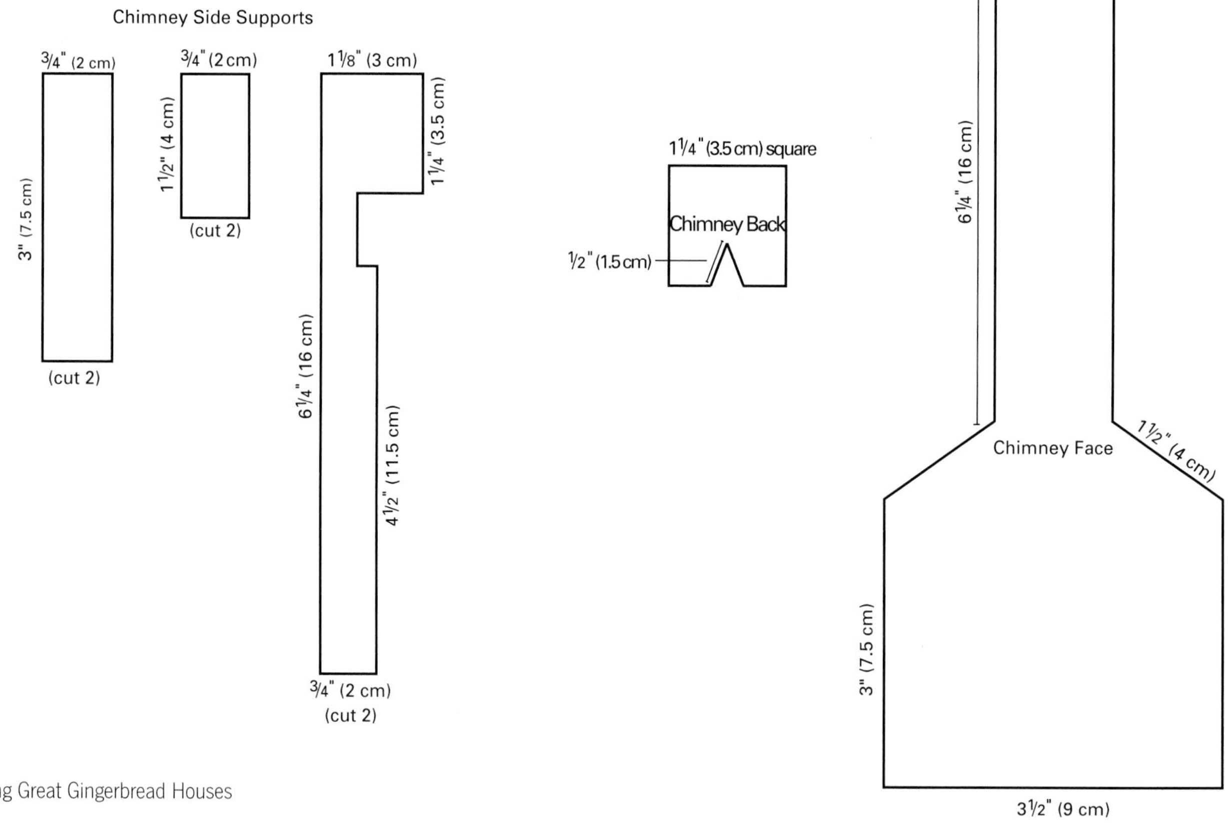

Chimney Side Supports

3/4" (2 cm)
3" (7.5 cm)
(cut 2)

3/4" (2 cm)
1 1/2" (4 cm)
(cut 2)

1 1/8" (3 cm)
1 1/4" (3.5 cm)
6 1/4" (16 cm)
4 1/2" (11.5 cm)
3/4" (2 cm)
(cut 2)

1 1/4" (3.5 cm) square
Chimney Back
1/2" (1.5 cm)

1 1/4" (3.5 cm)
6 1/4" (16 cm)
Chimney Face
1 1/2" (4 cm)
3" (7.5 cm)
3 1/2" (9 cm)

Basic House

PIECES SHOWN AT 50%—ENLARGE 200%

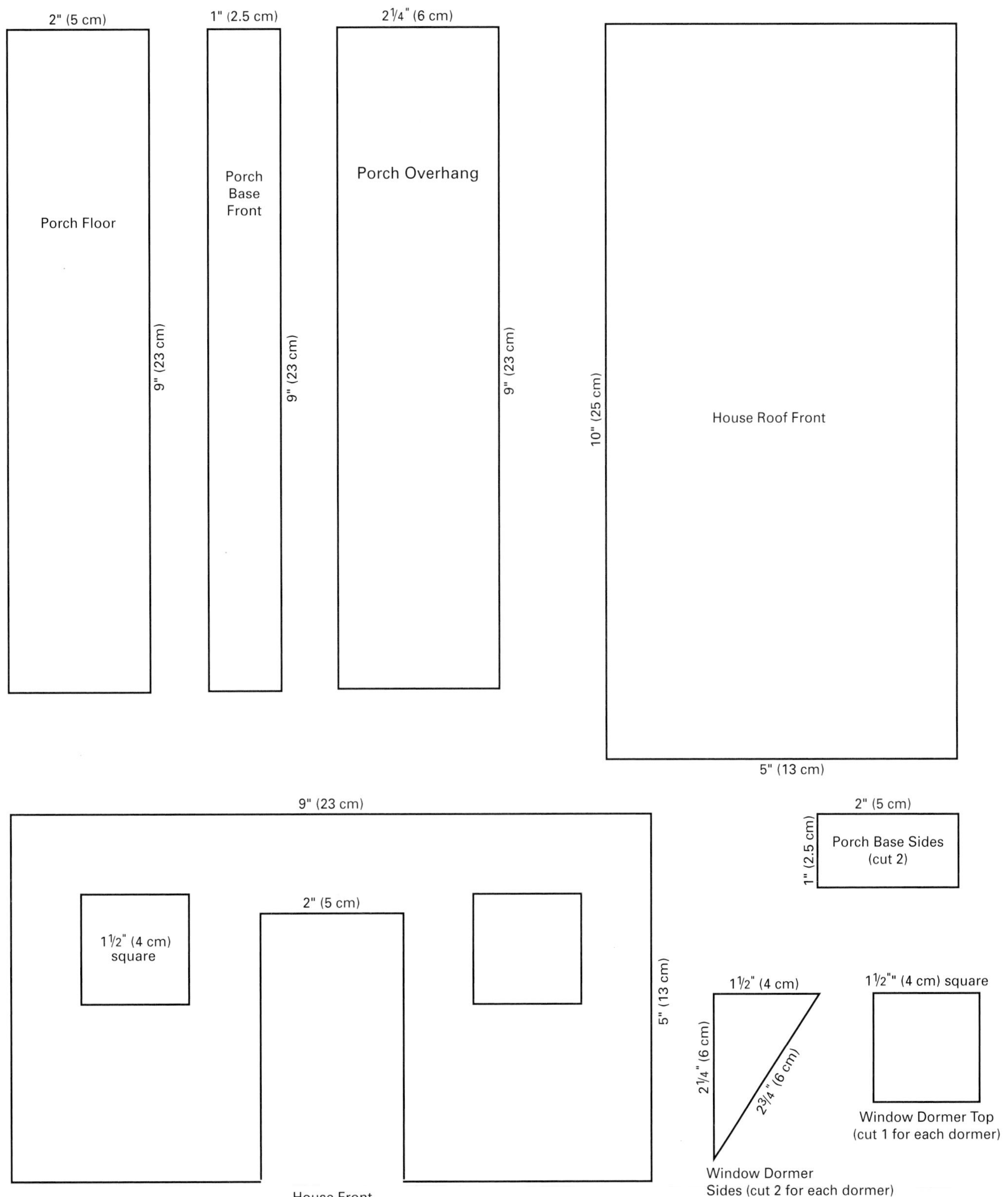

Basic House

PIECES SHOWN AT 50%—ENLARGE 200%

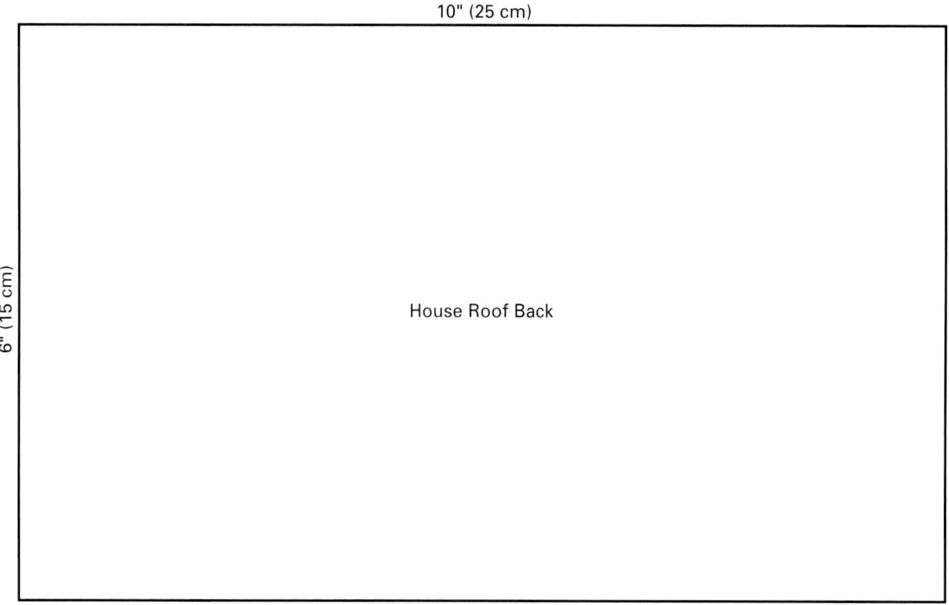

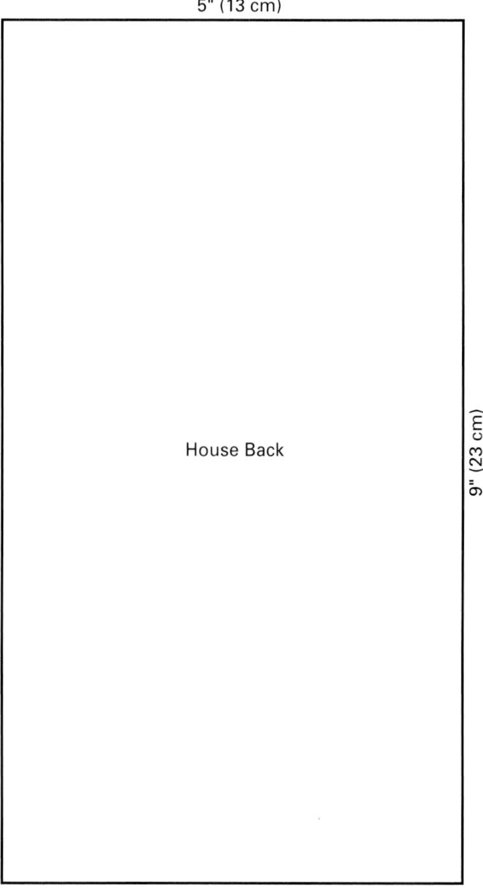

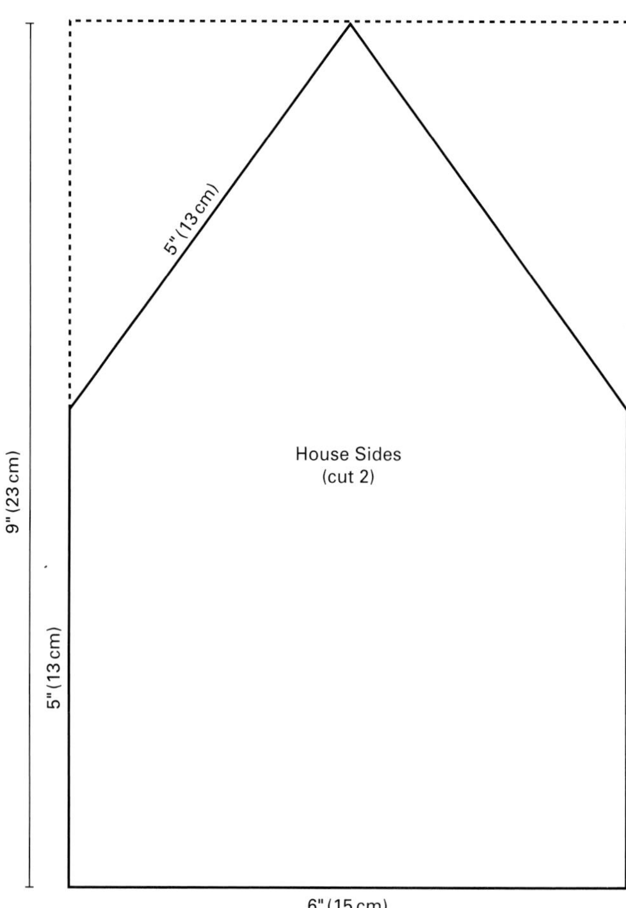

Tree House with a Twist

PIECES SHOWN AT 50%—ENLARGE 200%

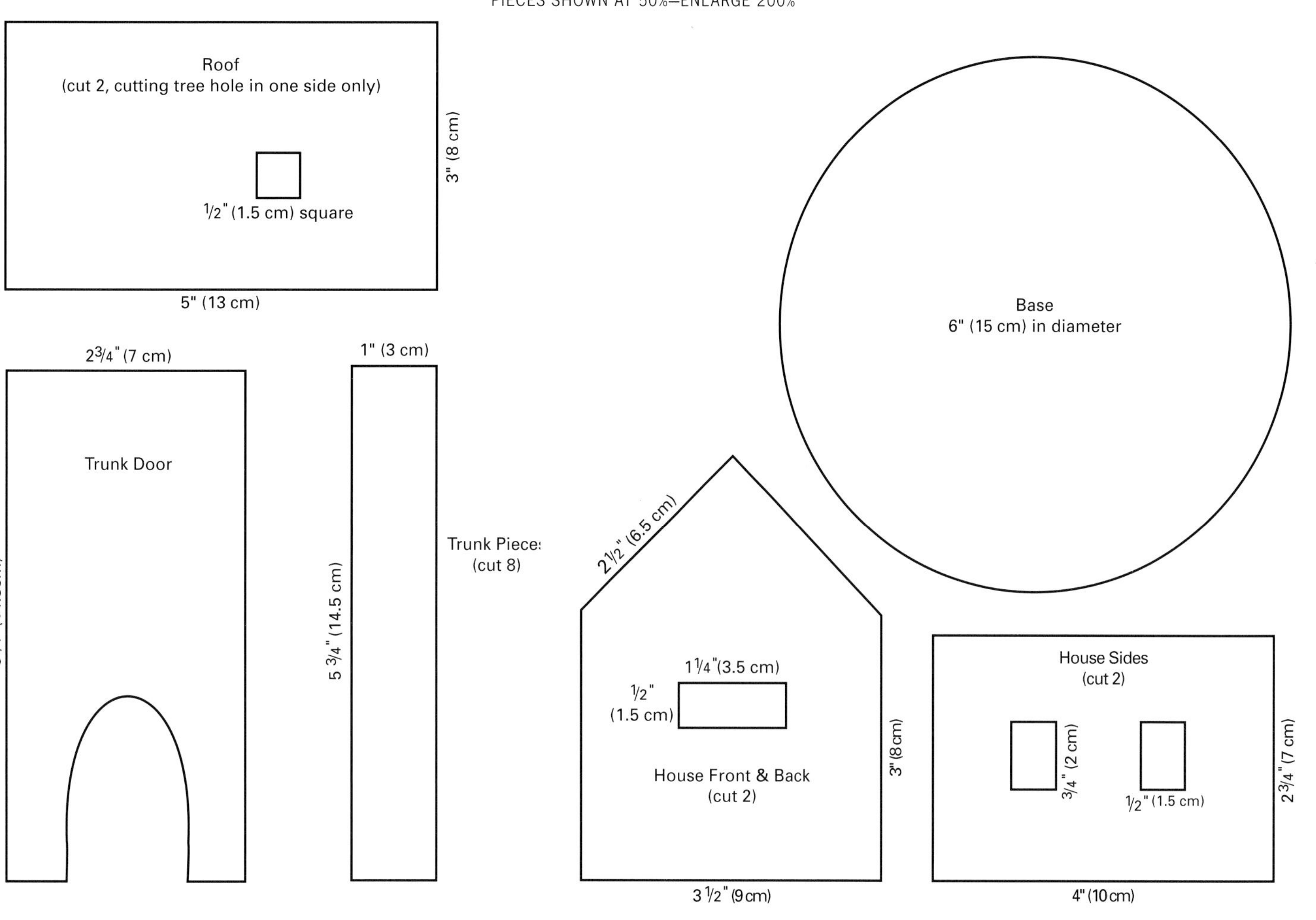

Sweetheart Cottage

SIGN AND BRIDGE

PIECES SHOWN AT 50%—ENLARGE 200%

7" (17.5 cm)

Bridge Sides
(cut 2)

3 3/4" (9.5 cm)

1" (2.5 cm)

7" (17.5 cm)

2" (5 cm)

Sign Bases
(cut 2)

Sign
(cut 2)

1" (2.5 cm)

Christmas Wedding Chapel

STEEPLE

PIECES SHOWN AT 50%—ENLARGE 200%

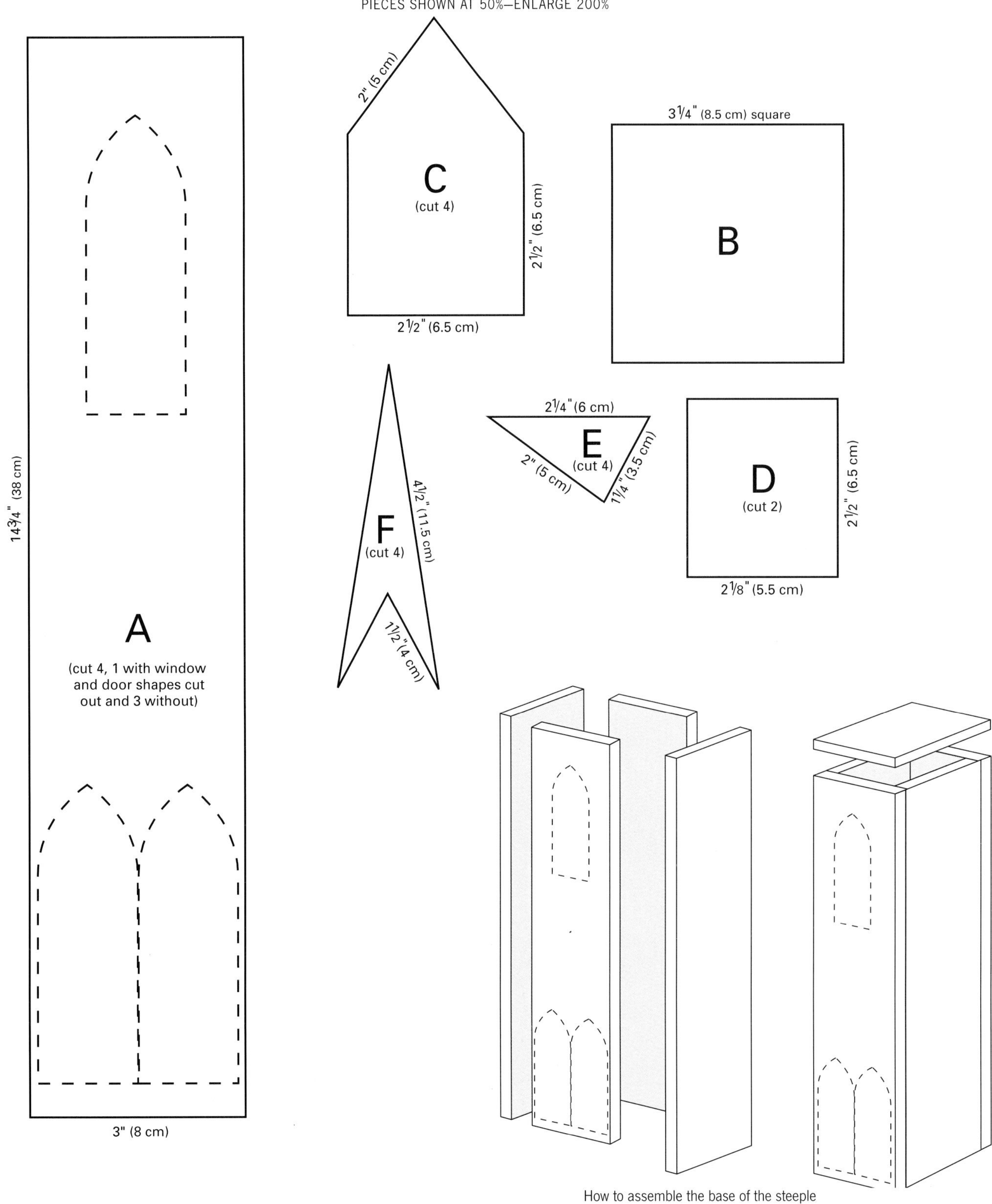

How to assemble the base of the steeple

Christmas Wedding Chapel

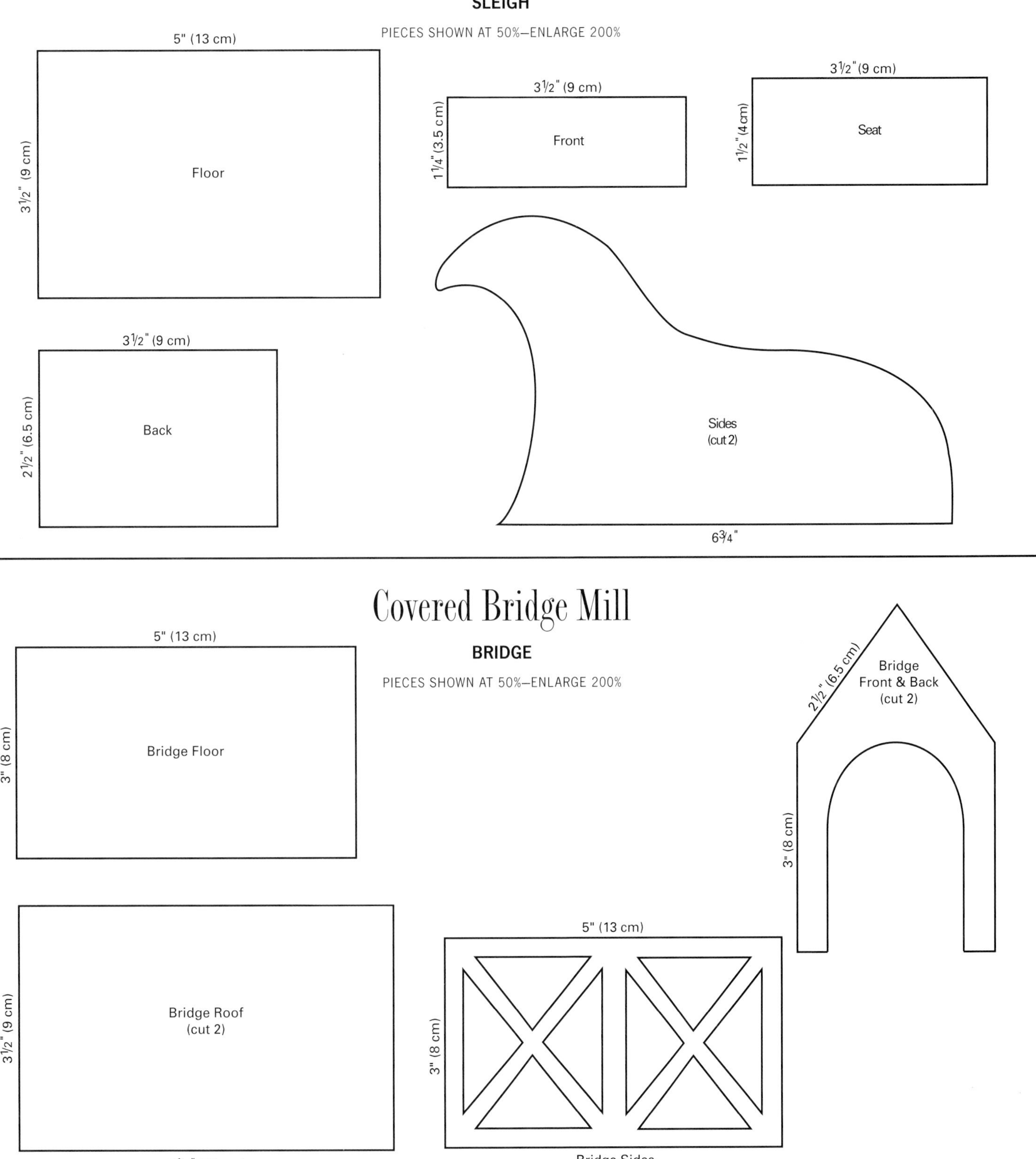

Fire House Christmas

FIRE WAGON

PIECES SHOWN AT 100%—NO ENLARGEMENT NECESSARY

5" (13 cm)
2¼" (6 cm)
Bottom
2¼" (6 cm)
Driver's Seat
½" (1.5 cm)
1¼" (3.5 cm)
Sides (cut 2)
Wheels
(cut 4)
2½" (6.5 cm) in diameter
Harness
(cut 2)
4½" (11.5 cm)
before bent

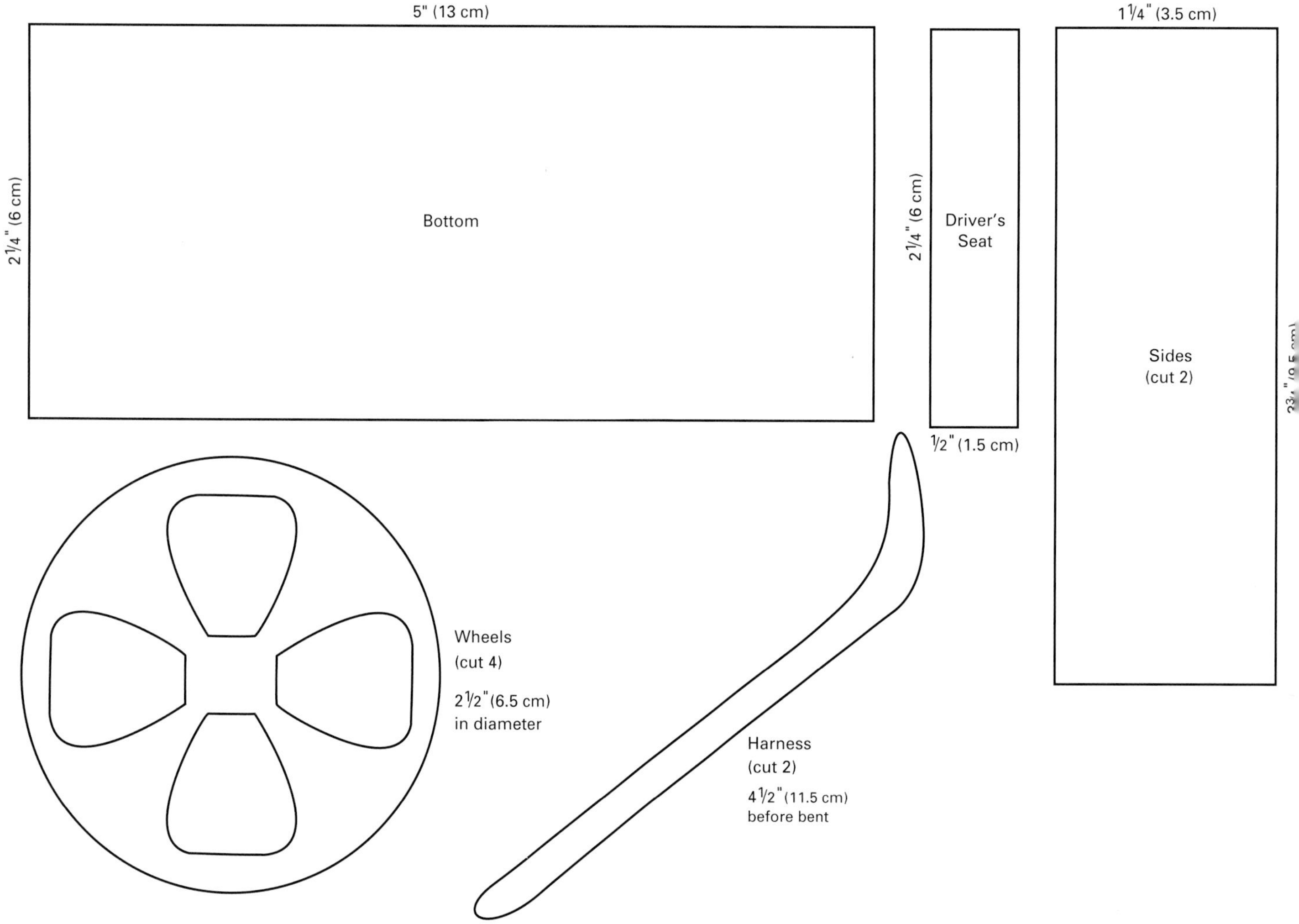

Little Red School House

SCHOOL BUS

PIECE SHOWN AT 100%—NO ENLARGEMENT NECESSARY

3" (8 cm)
¼" (1 cm) square
2" (5 cm)

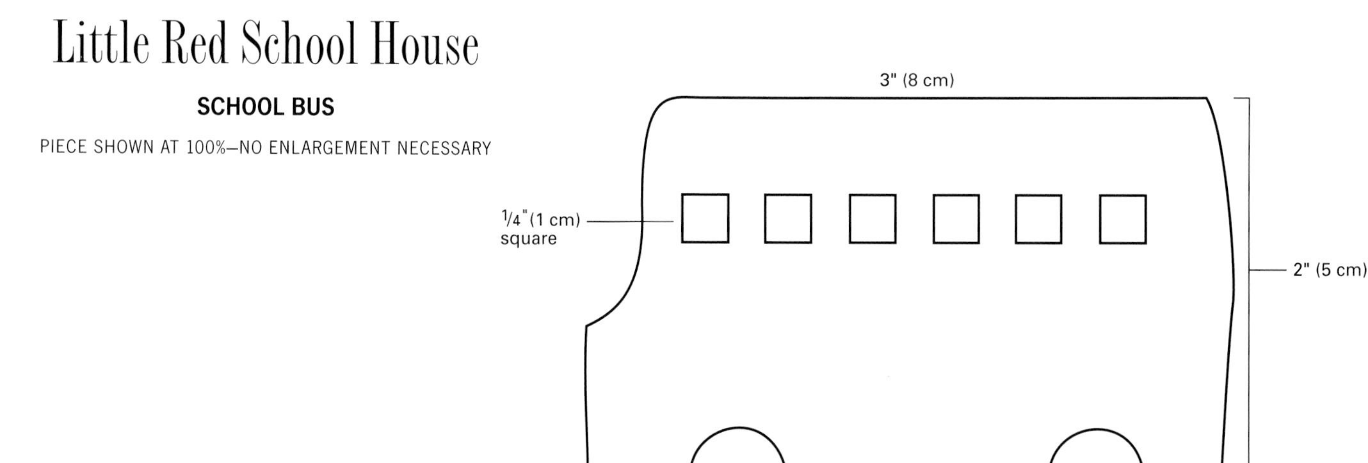

Holiday Village

LAMPPOST

PIECES SHOWN AT 100%—NO ENLARGEMENT NECESSARY

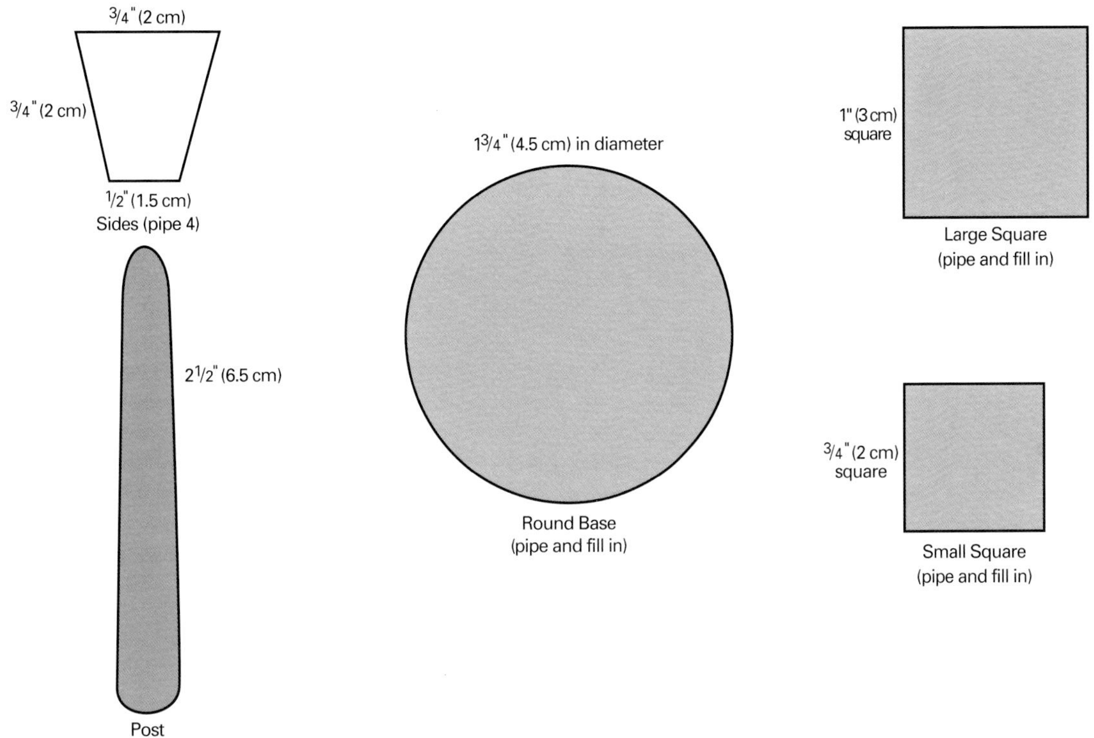

Down By the Old Mill Stream

WATER WHEEL

PIECE SHOWN AT 50%—ENLARGE 200%

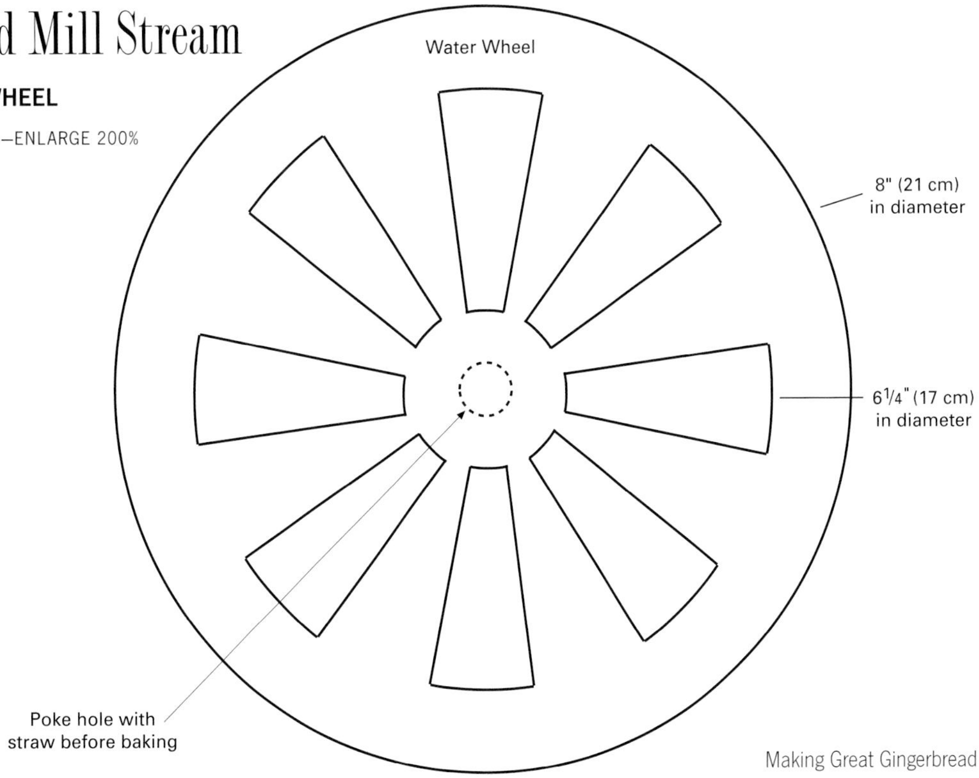

Water Wheel

8" (21 cm) in diameter

6 1/4" (17 cm) in diameter

Poke hole with straw before baking

Snow-covered Cottage

PIECES SHOWN AT 50%—ENLARGE 200%

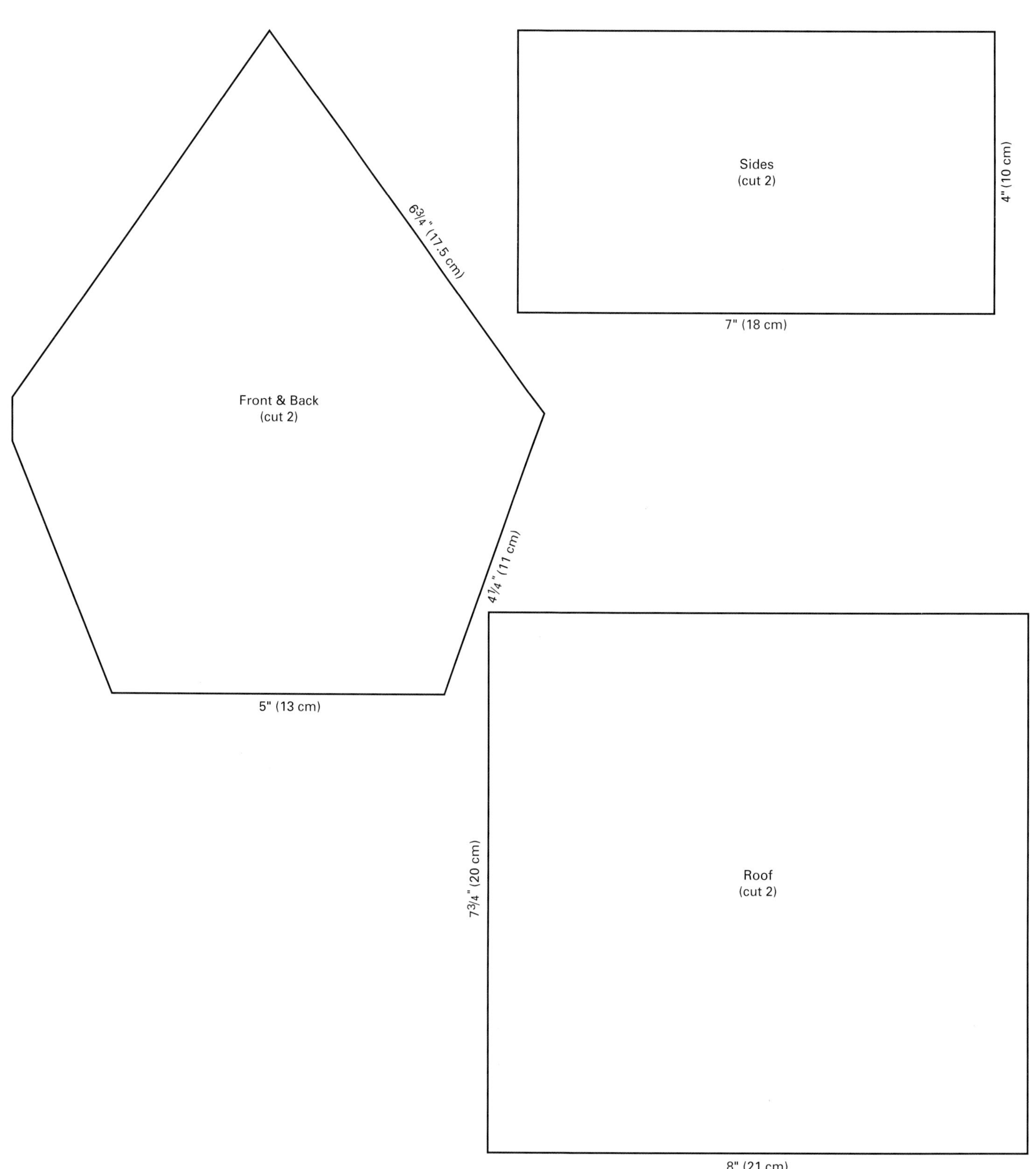

Stonecreek Inn

STAGECOACH AND HORSES

PIECES SHOWN AT 100%—NO ENLARGEMENT NECESSARY

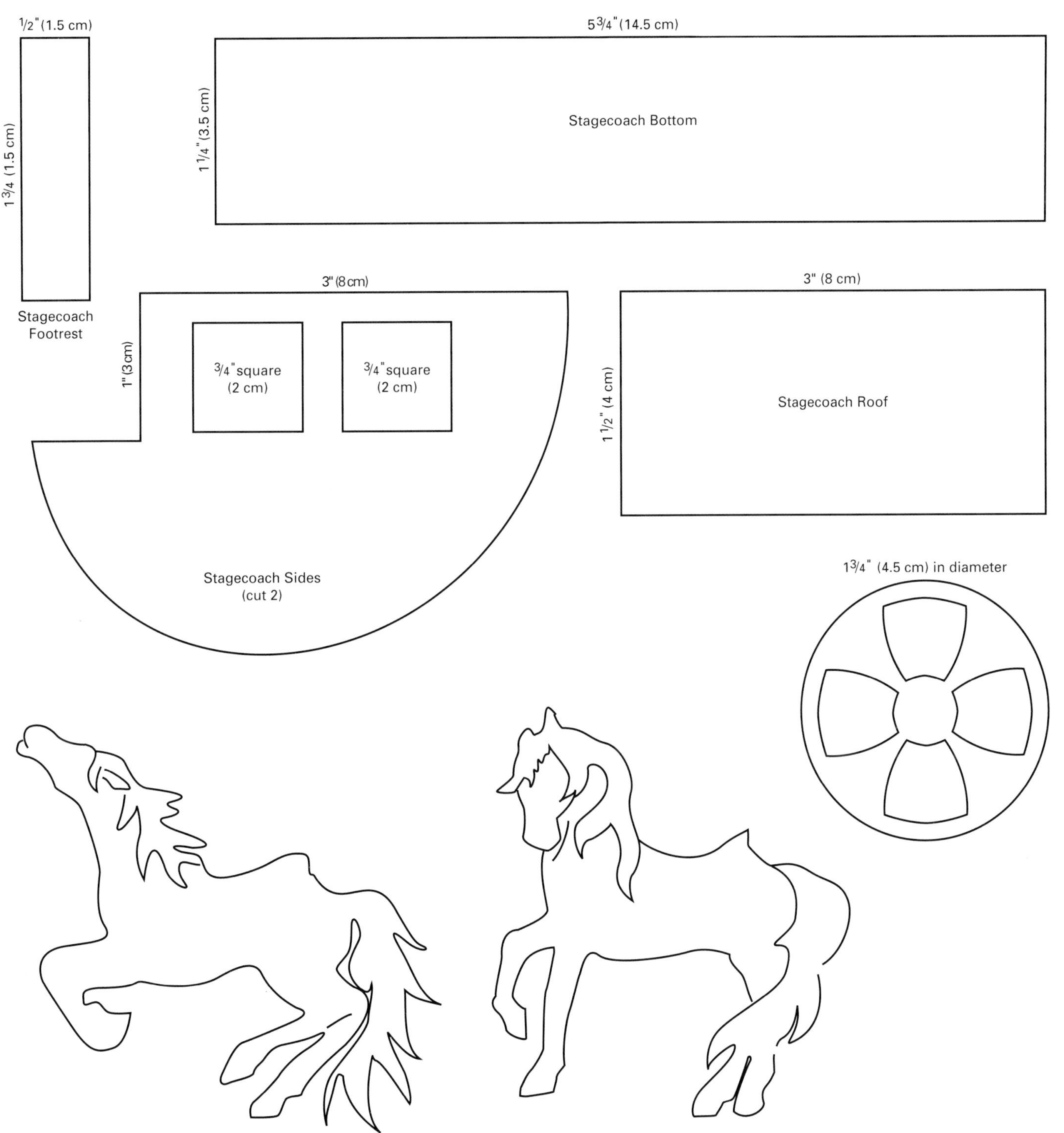

Hendersonville Depot

TOWER

PIECE SHOWN AT 50%—ENLARGE 200%

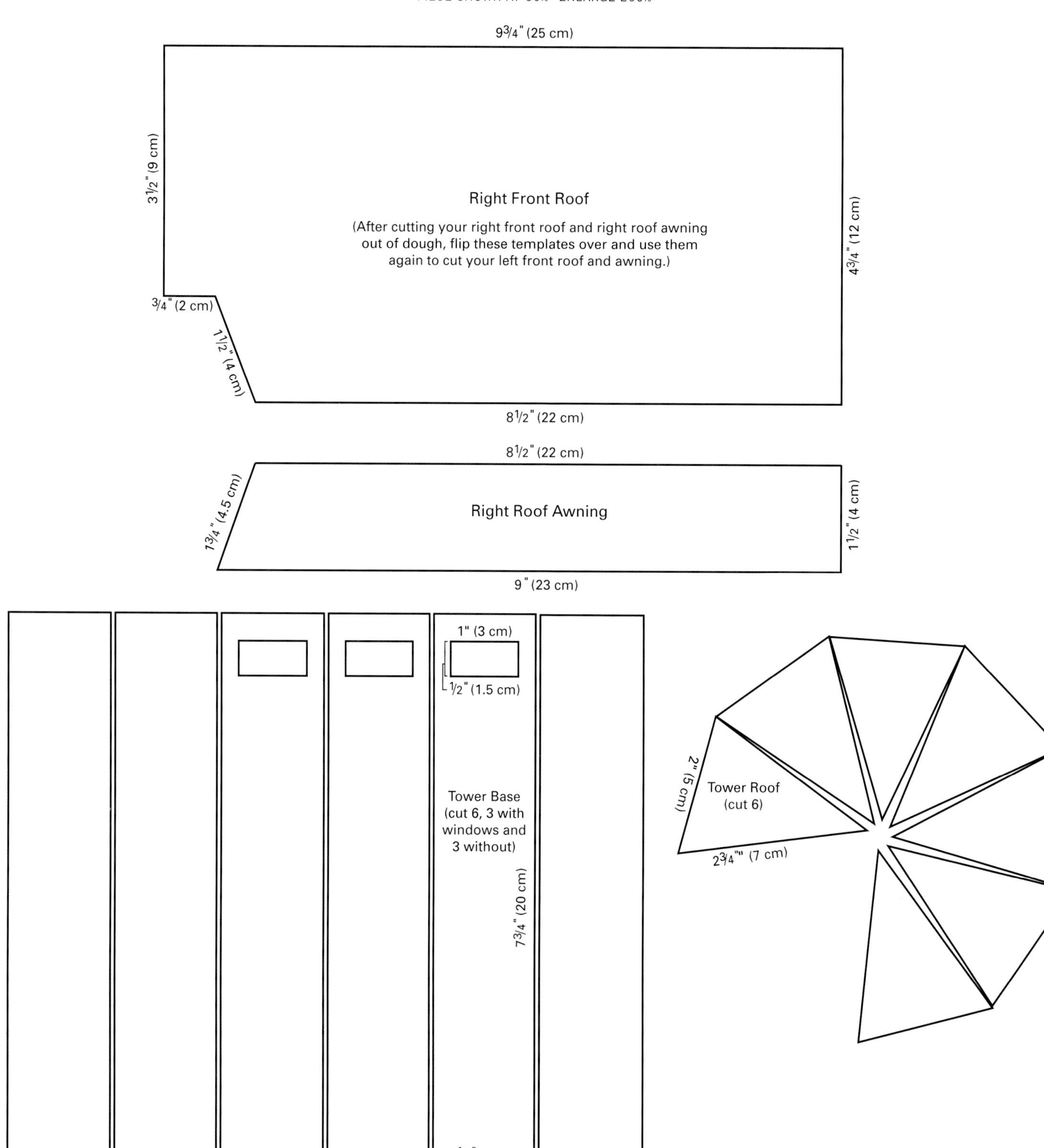

Zookeeper's Paradise

REPTILE HOUSE / AVIARY BASE

PIECE SHOWN AT 50%—ENLARGE 200%

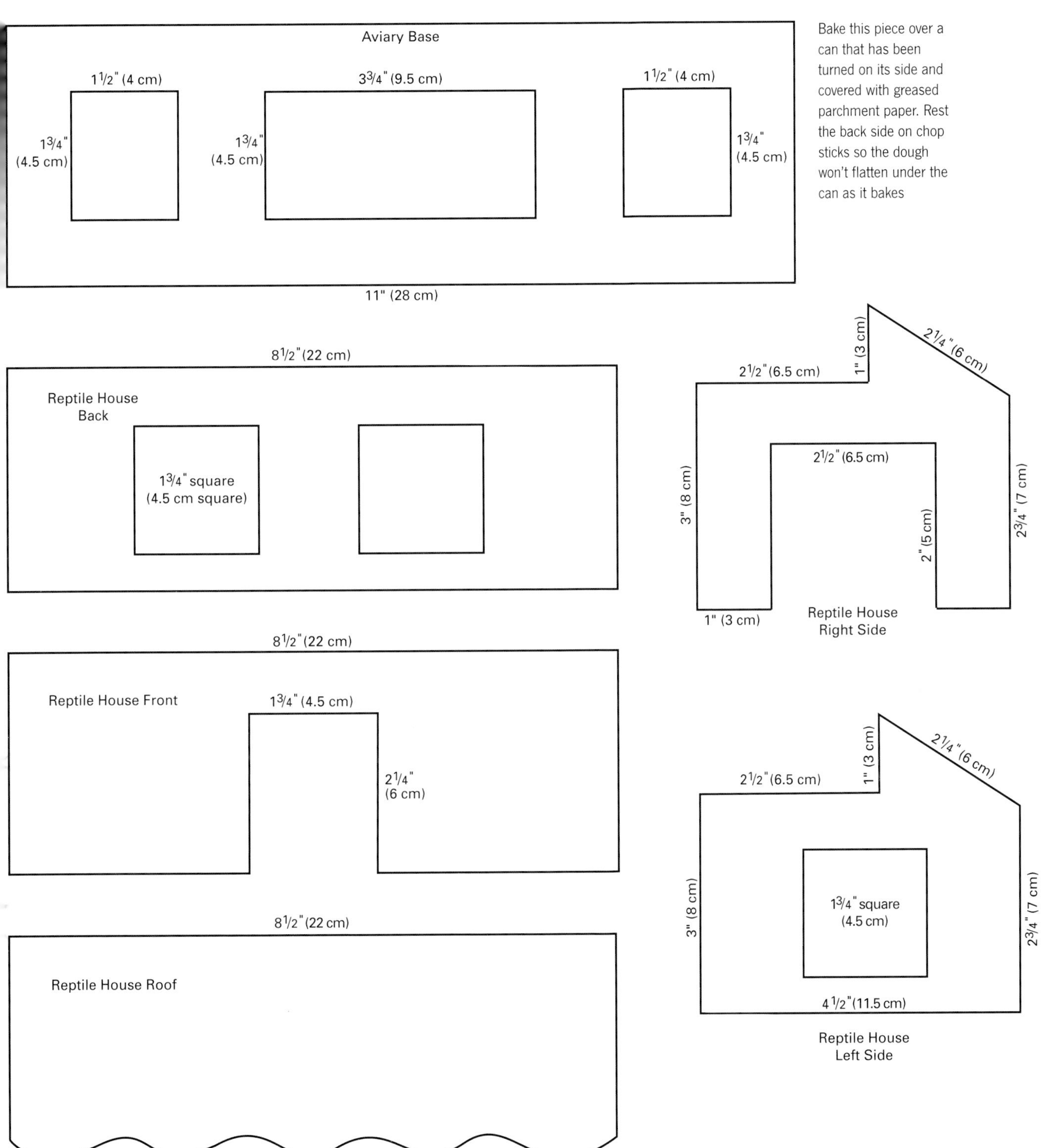

Bake this piece over a can that has been turned on its side and covered with greased parchment paper. Rest the back side on chop sticks so the dough won't flatten under the can as it bakes

Contributing Designers

TENLEY RAE ALAIMO has been constructing gingerbread sculpture for eight years. She prefers non-traditional subject matter and bakes several entries a year for various competitions.

DEREK ALDRIGE, **MARQUIS BROOKS**, and **KELLY TOBIN** have all completed a two-year high school culinary arts program at the Career and Technology Center in Williamston, SC. Each plans to pursue a career in the food industry.

ELIZABETH ASCIK, 15, loves both Christmas and baking. Making gingerbread houses combines the two interests perfectly.

BILL BENA is a versatile artist who works in many mediums, including oil painting, clay sculpture, airbrushing, and baking. After completing cooking school in New York, he worked in various bakeries. He has created gingerbread houses as Christmas gifts for years.

ELEANOR BERRY's design expertise focused primarily on appliquéd quilts and polymer clay jewelry until she entered the Grove Park Inn Gingerbread House Competition. Now, she has many more house ideas in the works and can't help but look for edible decorating possibilities every time she goes shopping.

MARGARET BRADSHAW entered her first gingerbread house contest in 1994, and has created something from dough and icing every year since. Every season, she pulls out all the equipment necessary to transform her kitchen and dining room into a gingerbread production studio.

BRIDGET BROCHU is the pastry chef at Biltmore Forest Country Club in Asheville, NC. She considers making a gingerbread house a challenging task and a work of art.

PHILLIP, **VICKIE**, **NOAH**, and **LINDSEY CAPPS** spent years viewing others' gingerbread houses, longing to create their own. They finally turned their dream into a reality (and a fun family project) and hope to make it a holiday tradition.

KRISTEN COOK, who enjoys cake decorating and other creative arts, built her first gingerbread house in 1993 at age 13. She entered it in the first Grove Park Inn Competition and has been the only participant to continue to enter every year since. Her houses have received numerous awards and much media coverage.

CERETTA DAVIS coordinates the Culinary Technology Program at Southwestern Community College in Sylva, NC. She directs first- and second-year students in collaborating on a gingerbread creation each fall.

HOBEY FORD, a professional touring puppeteer, creates dragons of a different nature when he isn't making gingerbread dragons with his daughter and sister-in-law.

LAUREN FORD is a high school home-schooler who loves acting in regional theatre productions when she isn't applying icing to gingerbread.

DEBRA ROBERTS teaches African dance and produces independent films with her Heron Productions, but also enjoys a cup of tea with family while creating gingerbread wonders.

SALLY FREDRICKSON's interests include art, decorating, and gourmet cooking. Gingerbread houses have become her way to have fun with all three. She's made houses for her family and for charities for more than a decade.

LISA GOELZ considers herself a newcomer to gingerbread art, but finds it both enjoyable and rewarding. She plans to make building houses and entering competitions a holiday tradition.

CATHERINE GONZALES has delighted family and friends with her custom-decorated cookies and cakes for many occasions and celebrations over the years. Her birdhouse complex was her first attempt at a gingerbread house, and now she's hooked.

KAREN GRAHAM enjoys both crafts and cooking, and likes making gingerbread houses because they combine the two hobbies. Her schoolhouse, featured in this book, is her third gingerbread creation.

LINDA HAFLER has been making gingerbread houses since 1996, some for home decorations and others to enter in contests. In 1997, she won third place in the Grove Park Inn Competition.

DAVID HANDERMANN entered his first gingerbread house competition in 1995 and went on, at age 14, to win first place in the youth category in the 1997 Grove Park Inn Competition. Despite the time and effort involved in making gingerbread houses, he enjoys the challenge.

MISTI HENDERSON and **MELISSA KIRK** are enrolled in a two-year high school culinary arts program at the Career and Technology Center in Williamston, SC.

JAMIE HICKS has completed a two-year high school culinary arts program at the Career and Technology Center in Williamston, SC, and plans to pursue a career in the culinary field. House-building partner **CASEY MASTERS** is a student in the same high school program.

PAM JOHNSON began her gingerbread house career in 1987 with her son's pre-school, making houses out of graham crackers with milk cartons as the base. She started baking her own gingerbread and creating one-room cottages in 1995, then built her way toward larger houses.

KATRA JOHNSON and **GINGER SMITH** are enrolled in a two-year high school culinary arts program at the Career and Technology Center in Williamston, SC. Though she enjoys food, Katra plans to pursue a career in child care (where she may become known as the care provider with the best snacks). Ginger credits her grandmother with helping her develop much of her cooking and baking expertise.

TYMBER LEWIS LANCE, six, has been in several different contests, but says he likes gingerbread contests best. His favorite part is seeing his house on display.

MELISSA LANCE has been decorating cakes for more than 13 years. She attempted her first gingerbread house in 1996. Gingerbread house building has been a holiday tradition in her home since.

JAMES MARSHALL, seven, thinks putting the gingerbread house pieces together is the best part of the house-making process. His mother says, truth be told, eating the candy as he works is actually his favorite part.

JULIA MARSHALL, 12, loves making and decorating cakes, so she suspected she might really enjoy creating gingerbread houses. She tried it, and she was right. Now she can't wait to make one every year.

SAM MARSHALL, nine, applied his interest in making and building things to gingerbread. He planned his first house a year in advance and found the process "hard but fun."

THOMAS MARSHALL and **JAMIE MERRITT** have both completed a two-year high school culinary arts program at the Career and Technology Center in Williamston, SC.

LAUREY C. MASTERTON is the owner of Laurey's Catering, Inc., which has been in operation in Asheville, NC, since 1987. The youngest daughter of Blueberry Hill Cookbook author Elsie Masterton, Laurey, outside of playing with gingerbread and candy, is an accomplished cook, teacher, traveler, and lover of wonderful foods.

TRISH MCCALLISTER has made gingerbread houses competitively and professionally since 1987. She has received numerous awards and honors, including Grand Prize at the Grove Park Inn Competition, which involved a guest appearance on "Good Morning America." She recently expanded into wedding cakes. She customizes them in her shop, The Cakery, in Spartanburg, SC.

Contributing Designers, continued

KATHY MOSHMAN has been decorating birthday, retirement, and going-away cakes since 1982, and has dabbled in wedding cakes and candy making. She's relatively new to gingerbread houses, but plans to continue to make them for many years to come.

ANNA OLSEN and her son **TODD**, 10, have explored craft projects together since Todd's early childhood. Todd is a master at making sculpy figures, a skill he transferred to marzipan to make animals for their gingerbread zoo.

ANTHONY PELLE, 10, spent several years decorating gingerbread houses with his mother and younger brother before creating one on his own. He chose a tree house theme because he's always wanted a real tree house, and thought decorating his creation was the best part.

KAREN POWELL has entered gingerbread houses in the Grove Park Inn Competition since 1995. With mood-setting Christmas music playing in the background, she begins planning her new house each October and enjoys the excitement of creating something different every year.

ELIZABETH M. PRIOLI's interest in gingerbread was sparked several years ago, after seeing a display of houses in Fort Wayne, IN. She has created many houses since, and always has one more she's dreaming about.

DREW ROWLAND, nine, started making gingerbread houses when he was five, but decided he needed a few years of practice before entering contests. At age eight, he began entering the Grove Park Inn Competition.

ALEX RUSSELL is an award-winning decorator who has been creating custom wedding and special-occasion cakes for eight years. After building gingerbread houses for five years, he entered his first gingerbread competition in 1997. He placed fifth at the Grove Park Inn Competition in 1998.

JUDY SEARCY teaches culinary arts at McDowell High School and has been decorating wedding and birthday cakes for more than 30 years. She has entered the Grove Park Inn Gingerbread House Competition every year since its inception in 1993, and she now hosts her own contest for her culinary arts students each December.

JUNE SMITH and **SHANON SMITH** are a mother-in-law/daughter-in-law gingerbread team. Before collaborating on their own house, they spent nearly a decade hosting house-building parties for Shanon's children and dozens of their friends.

TRACY L. SONIA is hooked on both Halloween and baking. She combined the two interests to create her haunted gingerbread house.

STEVEN, **DAVID**, and **SUZANNE UHLMAN**, ages 11, 7, and 6 respectively, got their inspiration for their first gingerbread house from a local train depot. They enjoyed both choosing and sampling their candy decorations.

EMILY GRACE YOUNG, 13, loves to create, period. Her hobbies include making jewelry at her dad's goldsmith/gem shop, drawing, pottery, clay sculpture, making banners, and, now, gingerbread house building.

Index